The EQ Way

Also by Ignacio Lopez

Keeping It Real and Relevant: Building Authentic Relationships in Your Diverse Classroom

The EQ Way

How Emotionally Intelligent School Leaders Navigate Turbulent Times

IGNACIO LOPEZ

Arlington, Virginia USA

2800 Shirlington Rd., Suite 1001 • Arlington, VA 22206 USA
Phone: 800-933-2723 or 703-578-9600 • Fax: 703-575-5400
Website: www.ascd.org • Email: member@ascd.org
Author guidelines: www.ascd.org/write

Richard Culatta, *Chief Executive Director*; Anthony Rebora, *Chief Content Officer*; Genny Ostertag, *Managing Director, Book Acquisitions and Editing*; Susan Hills, *Senior Acquisitions Editor;* Mary Beth Nielsen, *Director, Book Editing*; Jamie Greene, *Senior Editor*; Thomas Lytle, *Creative Director*; Donald Ely, *Art Director*; Daniela Aguero/The Hatcher Group, *Graphic Designer*; Cynthia Stock, *Typesetter*; Kelly Marshall, *Production Manager*; Shajuan Martin, *E-Publishing Specialist*; Christopher Logan, *Senior Production Specialist*; Kathryn Oliver, *Creative Project Manager*

Copyright © 2024 ASCD. All rights reserved. It is illegal to reproduce copies of this work in print or electronic format (including reproductions displayed on a secure intranet or stored in a retrieval system or other electronic storage device from which copies can be made or displayed) without the prior written permission of the publisher. By purchasing only authorized electronic or print editions and not participating in or encouraging piracy of copyrighted materials, you support the rights of authors and publishers. Readers who wish to reproduce or republish excerpts of this work in print or electronic format may do so for a small fee by contacting the Copyright Clearance Center (CCC), 222 Rosewood Dr., Danvers, MA 01923, USA (phone: 978-750-8400; fax: 978-646-8600; web: www.copyright.com). To inquire about site licensing options or any other reuse, contact ASCD Permissions at www.ascd.org/permissions or permissions@ascd.org. For a list of vendors authorized to license ASCD ebooks to institutions, see www.ascd.org/epubs. Send translation inquiries to translations@ascd.org.

ASCD® is a registered trademark of Association for Supervision and Curriculum Development. All other trademarks contained in this book are the property of, and reserved by, their respective owners, and are used for editorial and informational purposes only. No such use should be construed to imply sponsorship or endorsement of the book by the respective owners.

All web links in this book are correct as of the publication date below but may have become inactive or otherwise modified since that time. If you notice a deactivated or changed link, please email books@ascd.org with the words "Link Update" in the subject line. In your message, please specify the web link, the book title, and the page number on which the link appears.

PAPERBACK ISBN: 978-1-4166-3270-2   ASCD product #123046   n1/24
PDF EBOOK ISBN: 978-1-4166-3271-9; see Books in Print for other formats.
Quantity discounts are available: email programteam@ascd.org or call 800-933-2723, ext. 5773, or 703-575-5773. For desk copies, go to www.ascd.org/deskcopy.

Library of Congress Cataloging-in-Publication Data

Names: Lopez, Ignacio, 1979– author.
Title: The EQ way : how emotionally intelligent school leaders navigate
    turbulent times / Ignacio Lopez.
Description: Arlington, Virginia USA : ASCD, [2024] | Includes
    bibliographical references and index.
Identifiers: LCCN 2023040316 (print) | LCCN 2023040317 (ebook) | ISBN
    9781416632702 (paperback) | ISBN 9781416632719 (pdf ebook)
Subjects: LCSH: Educational leadership. | Emotional intelligence.
Classification: LCC LB2805 .L556 2024 (print) | LCC LB2805 (ebook) | DDC
    371.2/011—dc23/eng/20231017
LC record available at https://lccn.loc.gov/2023040316
LC ebook record available at https://lccn.loc.gov/2023040317

---

30 29 28 27 26 25 24   1 2 3 4 5 6 7 8 9 10 11 12

The EQ Way

How Emotionally Intelligent
School Leaders
Navigate Turbulent Times

Foreword _____ vii

Introduction _____ 1

CHAPTER 1
Improving Your Emotional Intelligence During Difficult Times _____ 9

CHAPTER 2
Emotions and the Clarity of Your Vision
During Difficult Times _____ 24

CHAPTER 3
Creating and Leading Emotionally Intelligent Teams _____ 40

CHAPTER 4
Increasing the Emotional Intelligence of Your School Culture _____ 50

CHAPTER 5
Emotional Intelligence and External Stakeholder Engagement _____ 65

CHAPTER 6
Navigating Naysayers and Resisters During Difficult Times _____ 77

CHAPTER 7
Sustaining and Scaling Emotional Intelligence in Schools _____ 90

References _____ 102

Index _____ 111

About the Author _____ 114

Foreword

The answer is "yes." The question could be any variation of the following: *Does emotional intelligence really matter? Will these strategies help me become a stronger leader? Do the "soft skills" of human interactions make a difference? Do I really need to read this book?*

I've known Dr. Ignacio Lopez for well over a decade, during which time his skills and savvy have repeatedly impressed me. We met through conferences and committees at ASCD, and it was a no-brainer for Alisa Simeral and me to invite him to be a part of our Building Teachers' Capacity Cadre as a professional learning facilitator, providing professional development across the country for administrators, instructional coaches, and other school leaders.

In this book, Ignacio explores emotional intelligence—or EQ—something with which he's cultivated a significant amount of expertise. Over the years, the importance of fostering our EQ has become more and more essential. As Ignacio shares, it's grown from a "nice to have" skill to a "need to have" imperative if we're to effectively lead people through change, growth, struggles, or any other sort of challenging times.

And since I don't remember a time that leadership wasn't challenging, I'd say developing our EQ is critical always, in every situation, in all settings.

Always. Proactively. Deliberately. It's not an option to be emotionally intelligent because we're talking about leading people. And because people are driven first by emotion and then reason, it's logical to connect with, understand, and appeal to our people at that level. It's simply a matter of tending to the Human Element in our work as leaders, which Ignacio argues is the most important and impactful facet of our leadership responsibilities.

My own experiences as a school leader serve to amplify the message Ignacio shares. I've been the principal of three schools, all of which found themselves in an uphill battle toward success and each of which sat in a precarious situation of underachievement, strife, and undue external pressures. The accomplishments that followed were not the result of my extraordinary natural leadership abilities, my outlandish intelligence, or my vast knowledge of strategic planning and organizational management. Rather, our collective successes came after we grew together as a team, began to understand one another as human beings, and built an extensive network of connections. The humans in the equation all learned to work in concert with one another—first at the emotional level, then at the tactical level.

What I've found fascinating (and daunting) is that while Ignacio urges us to emphasize our EQ as a fundamental leadership approach, I recall educators and leaders I've known who have said, "I'm not really into the soft skills," "We've got more important things to do," "I'm not a touchy-feely type of leader," or something like that.

Is that you? Do you think of emotional intelligence as a frivolous attribute or perhaps as something that a rare few people are endowed with at birth?

Good news! Over the course of this book, you'll uncover that EQ is a learnable, developable skill. You can get better at it, and Ignacio will show you how! Further, he offers strategies and approaches to help you develop the EQ of your schools, teams, and boards of education. You'll learn about the keys of open communication, clarity of vision, presence of shared values, and opportunities to build a network of committed stakeholders.

Remember, as a leader, *it's not about you.* It's about your people. EQ is simply a set of attitudes, behaviors, and strategies that promote that reality as a priority, so you and your school community can thrive through tough times (and, remember, *always*).

As a reflective practitioner, I'm impressed (and not at all surprised) by Ignacio's insertion of self-reflective questions throughout the text. I encourage you to take advantage of these prompts by pausing, reflecting, maybe even journaling or exchanging thoughts with a trusted colleague, and determining a plan of action to move forward with confidence and a strategic mindset.

Do you want to be an amazing leader? Would you like to develop your emotional intelligence? Are you interested in connecting more tightly with your people? Will you have an incredible impact on your school community? Is it time to strive toward excellence?

The answer is "yes."

—Pete Hall
former teacher, principal, and author of six ASCD books, including *Creating a Culture of Reflective Practice*

Introduction

In the fall of 2017, Superintendent Erin Smith found herself at a crossroads with her community. Over the past few months, parents had been showing up to school board meetings by the dozens demanding answers about elementary school special education programming in the district. They felt as though services needed improvement, special education teachers were doing a poor job, and the school counselors were underperforming in their duties. Instead of feeling like their children were being seen, understood, educated, and supported, parents received letters from the school and district saying their children would not be able to receive the services they needed. They were angry—and as members of a multilingual and multicultural community, they were also afraid and unsure of how to respond. They perceived the principal and superintendent as cold, unwelcoming, and culturally insensitive. When they set foot in their children's school, they felt as though they were treated as nuisances.

The superintendent's strategy was usually to wait out these kinds of complaints. Most of the time they faded away—but not this time. Though parents' letters and public comments to the board had initially focused on questions about the special education program and district leaders' conduct, they soon turned into demands for change. When Superintendent Smith's contract came up for renewal around this time, she was shown the door.

Why did things have to end this way for Superintendent Smith? I boil it all down to emotional intelligence. Leaders experiencing and facing hardships, conflict, and division must learn to navigate these situations with a level head. Contrary to stereotypes, emotionally intelligent leadership doesn't mean leading with weakness but rather keeping your strength under control.

Twenty-five years ago, leaders were expected to "bigfoot" through problems, their attitude and confidence towering over staff despite little knowledge of what was happening on the ground. Superintendents can't get away with that kind of behavior any longer. Research increasingly shows that higher levels of emotional intelligence, or EQ, predict greater organizational success (Batool, 2013; Doe et al., 2015; Goleman, 2014; Krén & Séllei, 2021).

Superintendent Smith took critical public comments as an attack on her personally rather than on the position. Instead of leaning into parents' concerns to discover and unpack their experiences, she became defensive. To the community, it felt as though Smith had stepped back and put a barricade around herself—and that the teachers were willing to join her. Rather than fostering an environment of success, unity, and learning, Smith had fostered an adversarial one with administrators and faculty on one side and parents on the other.

I have seen Superintendent Smith's experience repeated over and over across the United States. I have also studied and learned from education leaders who grasp the need for emotionally intelligent learning environments. As leaders, we can expect to find ourselves in difficult situations with students and their families. Navigating these situations can cause us anxiety and worry, leading us to react rather than decipher, decide, and lead. Understanding how our own emotions, thoughts, and awareness can influence our decisions and leadership style is essential to navigating difficult situations successfully. After all, we are not leading schools for our own sake but as servant leaders who take the lives of children and families into our own hands every day.

Leaders who learn how to master the five dimensions of EQ or emotional intelligence—self-awareness, self-regulation, motivation, empathy, and social skills (Goleman, 1995)—and who help foster these domains in their schools will find success in their leadership and with their students. We don't have to let every situation lead to conflict or division. As leaders, we can control our reactions in the moment, preventing our own impatience or misinterpretations from creating unwarranted difficulties.

In her study on high-conflict situations, Amanda Ripley (2021) states that institutions can be designed to promote either conflict or unity. Everything from politics to business can be seen or interpreted as a contest between "winners" and "losers," but in the education space, the only winners should be our students, and our leadership should be about promoting unity rather than conflict. Although leaders may want to come across as mediators in our schools, the nature of our position and title automatically puts us on the side of the administration. How we see ourselves, carry ourselves, react, and communicate inevitably define us in the eyes of students and their families. In difficult times, these perceptions are especially important—and so, too, is emotional intelligence.

When the negative happens, or the frightful, or the unknown—when we're confused because we aren't sure where things are headed—that's when a focus on emotional intelligence needs to surface. It's why a book like this is necessary: to help point out when, where, and possibly how school leaders can navigate difficult situations by leveraging their emotional intelligence.

Level-headed and emotionally intelligent leaders keep their attention on service, on student learning, and on keeping children and their families safe. The difficulties that make their way into our schools can be related to national issues such as the economy, political polarization, fake news, and racial tensions or on local issues such as union negotiations, layoffs, and violence in the community. There will always be a correlation between these difficulties and our actions, reactions, and emotions as leaders.

The strategies and ideas in this book are meant to inspire reaction and reflection. As you read through each chapter, challenge your own approach to leadership. Ask yourself, "How can I 'get better at getting better' at using my emotional intelligence (EQ) to navigate challenges in my school?" and "How can I help foster a more emotionally intelligent school community so we can all successfully navigate challenges together?"

My research and experience have led me to identify the following seven characteristics that emotionally intelligent school leaders have in common when facing challenges in their buildings or communities:

1. Defining, understanding, and being curious about improving their emotional intelligence in high-conflict situations.
2. Continually assessing the clarity of their vision and communication.

3. Forming teams and enforcing norms of engagement and accountability across the school community.
4. Refining, communicating, and monitoring school values.
5. Deliberately and continually engaging with both internal and external stakeholders.
6. Finding ways to both work with and stand up to naysayers and resisters.
7. Purposely growing the emotional intelligence of the school community.

Each chapter in this book focuses on one of these characteristics and includes both case studies and strategies that readers can try for themselves or reflect on with their teams:

- Chapter 1 introduces Daniel Goleman's research on emotional intelligence and provides a set of strategies leaders can use to develop emotional intelligence in themselves and their staff. The reflection questions at the end of this chapter challenge leaders to dig deep into their areas of strength and weakness in each of the five domains of emotional intelligence.
- Chapter 2 explores the importance of having a vision and a way to communicate it, and it offers strategies for assessing the clarity of both in difficult times. The reflection questions at the end of this chapter challenge school leaders to reflect on their current vision and think about how current team members may have contradictory views of their vision.
- Chapter 3 focuses on the characteristics of emotionally intelligent teams. Here, you'll find strategies for setting

team norms and examples of when and how to create successful teams. The reflection questions at the end of the chapter challenge leaders to think about the health, success, and engagement levels of team members in their schools.
- Chapter 4 shares the story of a principal navigating racial tensions in his school and community, showing how he led a team of teachers in assessing and monitoring their school values. The reflection questions in this chapter challenge leaders to think about how their current school values can assist or deter them in overcoming difficult situations.
- Chapter 5 shares trends in community school engagement and strategies for effectively engaging with external stakeholders during challenging times. This chapter also examines a real-life school's successful approach to community engagement during a time of turnaround. The reflection questions in this chapter challenge leaders to define their external and internal stakeholder groups and think through ways of improving engagement with emotional intelligence.
- Chapter 6 shares strategies for engaging with naysayers, resisters, and skeptics that are grounded in emotional intelligence and rooted in trust building. The reflection questions in this chapter challenge leaders to think about their own emotions as they engage with negative people in moments of confrontation and conflict.
- Chapter 7 offers strategies for deliberately fostering emotionally intelligent learning spaces. The reflection questions in this chapter challenge leaders to think deliberately about the growth of emotional intelligence in their schools and their role in sustaining it.

How to Use This Book

This book is meant to be a guide and reflection tool for leaders navigating difficult times in their schools. Though it is best to read the book chapter by chapter, some readers might find value in going directly to the chapter focused on the area in which they need immediate help. I recommend reflecting on the questions at the end of each chapter either by yourself or with a professional learning community. Talking out loud and sharing your thoughts and personal journey with others is a way to develop your self-awareness about how you handle tough situations.

The work of increasing your emotional intelligence takes time; it is a process, and there will be slip-ups. We should be in a constant state of curiosity, of wanting to learn, and of wanting to improve. The worst thing we can do as leaders is believe that we have mastered our emotional intelligence. This is never true; we can *always* get better at getting better.

1

Improving Your Emotional Intelligence During Difficult Times

Even though qualities traditionally associated with leadership such as intelligence, determination, and vision are required for success, they are insufficient. Effective leaders are also distinguished by a high degree of emotional intelligence in the form of self-awareness, self-regulation, motivation, empathy, and refined social skills. These qualities may sound "soft," but leadership development research has found direct ties between emotional intelligence and measurable organizational results (Bradberry & Greaves, 2009; Druskat & Wolff, 2001; Goleman, 1995; Goleman et al., 2002). What's more, in an era of continued and growing divisiveness, school leaders need to model how to effectively navigate turbulent situations while protecting the learning and development of all children.

The Five Dimensions of Emotional Intelligence

The Collaborative for Academic, Social, and Emotional Learning (CASEL) outlines five dimensions of social-emotional learning

(SEL) for children: self-awareness, self-management, responsible decision making, relationship skills, and social awareness. We can take these same dimensions and crosswalk them to leadership development using Goleman's (1995) five dimensions of emotional intelligence: self-awareness, self-regulation, motivation, empathy, and social skills.

School leaders often unpack Goleman's five dimensions of emotional intelligence with teachers and students without taking the time to consider what the dimensions could mean for us as well. After all, we can't help our teachers and students develop their emotional intelligence if we aren't committed to developing our own.

Self-Awareness

Self-awareness refers to a deep understanding of our own emotions, strengths, weaknesses, needs, and drives. School leaders with strong self-awareness are neither overly critical nor unrealistically hopeful; they are honest with themselves and others. At the same time, they recognize how their feelings affect other people and their performance. School leaders who are self-aware know to recognize and credit the emotional intelligence of others. Too often, leaders don't give self-awareness the attention it deserves.

In times of change or turbulence, there is often a sense of urgency, but good leaders know when to slow down to support and acknowledge their colleagues' emotions. We must not mistake candor about our feelings for softness, and we should respect staff who openly acknowledge their emotions. Sadly, some leaders misinterpret emotional intelligence and self-awareness as signs of not being "tough enough," so their staff tend to bottle up their emotions.

The most successful school leaders I have worked with take an intentional or deliberate approach to building self-awareness through meditating, relying on trusted friends (inside and outside the district), and getting regular feedback from teachers and colleagues:

- **Meditation:** Implementing meditation practices doesn't have to be formal or ritualistic. Regular moments of pause and reflection can help to improve your moment-to-moment awareness.
- **Relying on trusted friends:** None of us is altogether aware of how we come across to others. School leaders must rely on trusted friends to learn the honest truth. It is worthwhile to ask such friends for their candid and critical objective perspectives on decisions you are making or about to make.
- **Regular feedback from teachers and colleagues:** Once a year, I ask teachers, staff, and students to complete an anonymous online survey in which they tell me what I need to (1) start doing, (2) stop doing, and (3) keep doing. Answers to surveys such as this can help you reflect on your self-awareness development.

Self-Regulation

It is no secret that biological impulses drive our emotions. We cannot do away with negative emotions altogether, but we *can* do much to manage them. Self-regulation is the inner conversation we are always having with ourselves. School leaders who are in control of their feelings act reasonably and create an environment of trust and fairness in which disagreements are sharply reduced. Additionally, knowing how to regulate our emotions can mean the difference between embracing our jobs and burning out.

School leaders who are in control of their emotions are better able to roll with changes and navigate students and staff through tough times. When new challenges arise, they don't panic but rather stay calm, suspend judgment, and seek out information before moving forward. Like self-awareness, self-regulation does not get the respect it deserves. People who control their emotions are sometimes seen as lacking passion, and it is people with fiery temperaments who have often been thought of as "classic" leaders. Thankfully, this idea is dying out. In my experience, emotional outbursts and extreme displays of negative emotion work against school leaders.

To help keep emotions in check during times of crisis, it's a good idea to pause and reflect before reacting. Even doing this for as little as two minutes can make a big difference. I have seen principals in the middle of heated debates with parents suddenly stop and say, "I'm sorry, I need to step out for just one minute." They'd step out, collect themselves, then return to the conversation.

One key to effective self-regulation is knowing when you might be on the cusp of needing it. Being cognizant of your feelings and the physical symptoms—such as churning in your stomach, light-headedness, faster breathing, or panic attacks—of those feelings coming on can help you better self-regulate. For example, I once asked a principal why he kept a fidget spinner on his desk. "They help me, too," he said. "Not because I'm fidgety but because if I start to reach for this thing in the middle of a difficult conversation or meeting, I know I'm about to lose it." Reaching for the spinner was a sign for this leader that he needed to begin self-regulating.

Motivation

Good leaders are driven to achieve above and beyond expectations. The key word here is *achieve*: though plenty of people are motivated by external factors such as higher salaries or prestige, the best school leaders are driven by a deep desire to achieve. Many enter leadership positions because they want to make a difference in the lives of the children and the families they serve. School leaders who are driven to achieve are forever raising the performance bar not only for themselves but also for their students and the school as a whole. They set realistic targets, use data to show improvement, and continuously monitor their progress. In fact, seeing evidence of progress is itself motivating.

Empathy

Of the five dimensions of emotional intelligence, empathy is perhaps the most easily recognized. We have all felt the empathy of a sensitive teacher or friend or been struck by its absence in an unfeeling coach, mentor, or boss. Many people seem to believe that empathy is out of place amid the tough realities of school leadership—but empathy isn't mushiness; it simply means thoughtfully considering others' feelings (and the factors that may be driving those feelings) before making decisions.

School leaders who practice empathy are strong listeners. When meeting with teacher teams, students, or parents, putting down your phone and giving them your undivided attention will help you better understand and connect with them. Use "looping"—the practice of paraphrasing or repeating what you have heard before you speak—as an active listening strategy.

Another key to empathy is talking to people outside our usual social circle or encountering lives and worldviews very different from our own. Sometimes leaders get so caught up in believing their perspective is the only reality that they forget the circumstances other people find themselves in.

It is also important for leaders to praise empathy in others. I have seen school leaders take a moment out of their meetings to recognize the teachers on their teams whenever they help others achieve their goals. Too often, our attention sways toward the loudest and most negative voices in the room. Noticing the good around us can balance our attention and increase our empathy. The more we cultivate our own empathy and encourage it in others, the more we contribute to an overall culture of empathy in our school.

Social Skills

The first three dimensions of emotional intelligence—self-awareness, self-regulation, and motivation—can be classified as self-management skills. By contrast, the last two, empathy and social skills, concern our ability to manage relationships with others.

Leveraging social skills as a leader during difficult times is not just a matter of friendliness; it is about friendliness with a purpose. Socially skilled school leaders tend to have a wide circle of acquaintances and a knack for finding common ground and building rapport with people of all kinds. This doesn't mean being social all the time, but it does mean working on the assumption that nothing important gets done alone.

School leaders with robust social skills may sometimes appear not to be working when they really are. They may seem to be idly chatting in the hallways with people who don't appear connected to their jobs when in reality they are building relationships with neighborhood leaders or donors. These leaders don't think it makes sense to arbitrarily limit the number or type of relationships they have. They are continuously building bonds across the board because they know they may need help from those connections someday.

Knowing how to pick up on social cues in a social or work setting is another characteristic of leaders with strong social skills. Because these leaders can perceive and correctly interpret social cues, they know when they need to lift others up or help them out. Leaders who don't have this ability may display unsocial behaviors and make others feel uncomfortable, frustrated, or devalued.

Emotional Intelligence and Culturally Responsive School Leadership

As our schools become increasingly diverse, our students need increased exposure to and understanding of other cultures and identities—to sympathize and empathize, learn to coexist, excel together, and love. And we can't claim to be culturally relevant leaders if we are lacking emotional intelligence. If we truly believe that all children can learn, that all children are good, and that all children can be successful, then we must meet *every* child where they are and help them. This is key to ensuring equity and cultural responsiveness.

Culture is an undeniable part of everything we do as humans, and emotional intelligence allows us to share cultural values and norms with students. Every day, students enter school spaces with values and beliefs that may cause them to see the world differently than we do. These values and beliefs shouldn't be dismissed just because they are unfamiliar to us. This is why educators need to sharpen their own emotional intelligence and lead by example. We must be clear that we will not allow our students' cultural differences to be perceived as deficits. Our emotional intelligence sets the tone for the entire school, and our students will not develop their own emotional intelligence unless we lead by example and model what makes us culturally unique. The easiest way to model this behavior is by giving students time to share their experiences and by listening without being critical or judgmental. Follow-up questions typically lead to a genuine interest in and help develop a perspective of what it means to be from another culture.

There is increasing research on the connection between emotional intelligence and cultural responsiveness in our schools (Donahue-Keegan et al., 2019; Durlak et al., 2011; Jennings et al., 2020; Markowitz & Bouffard, 2020). According to the literature, teacher preparation programs need to teach educators to develop a culturally responsive lens through which to perceive students, curriculum, and themselves. The same is true for leaders.

There are two phases to culturally responsive work in schools: a discovery phase centered on the emotional intelligence dimensions of self-awareness and empathy, and an application phase for implementing strategies (as Figure 1.1 illustrates). Unfortunately, some individuals engage only with the application phase of this work in schools and ignore the discovery phase. Researchers such as Gay (2010), Hammond (2014), and Ladson-Billings (2021) note that moving toward an inclusive and culturally responsive school takes time and requires processes to discover and apply our own interpretations, beliefs, and development of EQ and cultural awareness.

Figure 1.1 identifies five key steps for creating culturally relevant schools across both the discovery and application phases.

One of the difficulties we face as school leaders, especially during difficult times, is to find the time and create the space to sit through, discover, and share our own epiphanies related to self-awareness and empathy. There is also little appetite among students, staff, and community in most schools to sit with us during these discovery processes. As leaders, we must work hard to instill

FIGURE 1.1

The Discovery and Application Phases of Culturally Responsive Work

	Discovery Phase		**Application Phase**
Step 1	**Develop self-awarenes.** Unpack your personal realities to become more in tune with students' lived experiences, and learn about your own emotional intelligence and areas of opportunity for improvement.	Step 3	**Create welcoming and trusting learning spaces.** Consider strategies for engaging students and staff in honest and uncomfortable conversations about cultural relevance or responsiveness; apply a culturally responsive lens to both the physical and emotional learning environments as well as the curriculum.
Step 2	**Develop empathy.** Reflect on how you influence the learning space and the effect your presence has on students; expand your curiosity of other groups, students, cultures, and so on.	Step 4	**Learn about the different cultures, languages, and learning modalities in the learning space.** Ask nonjudgmental questions about students' customs and traditions and about how they learn best. The more you know about your students, the more culturally responsive your curriculum and pedagogy can be.
		Step 5	**Communicate, sustain, measure, and celebrate diversity in the learning space.** Implement strategies for doing these things to keep cultural responsiveness alive in your school or classroom. Measure your cultural responsiveness through data and be willing to intervene where necessary to improve it.

a curiosity about self-awareness and empathy in everyone if we are to lead them successfully through tough times.

Leadership Behaviors for Navigating Challenges

When I was the young leader of a large community college, I was in my top-floor office one day when I suddenly smelled smoke. Before I knew it, all the fire alarms in our 14-story building were going off. Though I was frightened and nervous, I knew I needed to remain calm. Almost immediately, the head of security popped his head into my office. Together, we jumped into action, working the stairwells to ensure students were evacuating the building. When we finally reached the first floor, I waited for some students to exit through the back alley of the building. The head of security grabbed me and said, "No sir, you need to go out the front door." The front door was all the way on the other side, full of other students and staff trying to exit the building. "They need to see you leave," continued the head of security. "You need to assure folks that everything is fine. If you are not panicking, they won't panic either."

It turns out there was a small fire in the building, but it was restricted to the science classrooms and the fire department soon arrived, so everything was under control. There was no need to head to our off-campus crisis command center and no lives were at risk, but the community needed reassurance that everything was alright. Seeing me walk through the lobby, calm and cool on the outside, was reassuring to our students.

In a moment of crisis, a school leader's behavior can either be triggering or calming. For this reason, we should be mindful of our behaviors and reactions to the behaviors of others. The school community expects us (1) to offer comfort and assurance that things will be OK—what psychologists refer to as "holding" or "holding space" (Slochower, 2013), (2) to mind our mood through self-regulation, and (3) to realistically communicate what is happening.

Holding Space

When things get tough or tensions rise, good leaders know how to see their entire school or district as one and interpret its overall "system anxiety." A school's system anxiety can be understood or interpreted as a collective feeling of unease or fear among teachers and staff members concerning the turbulent situation. This anxiety could be caused by various factors such as unclear processes, a lack of communication, inadequate resources, or a resistance to change. The idea of "holding" or "holding space," first introduced by psychologist D. W. Winnocott (Slochower, 2013), is simple. Just as parents hold their children close to their chest when they are sad and afraid, school leaders must "hold" their staff, students, and community close in times of crisis. Of course, I'm not talking about physically holding or hugging someone (though that can help, too) but rather creating a space where people feel that their feelings are valued and their anxieties understood.

Holding institutional space, because of system anxiety, as a leader includes reassuring teachers and staff about their job security, about the decisions they can make about curriculum or professional development, and about whether they are being treated fairly. In my experience, teachers and staff during turbulent times are primarily concerned with what will happen to their jobs. They are then most concerned about the grade levels they are going to teach (i.e., Will they keep teaching the same grade or change to a different level?) and the need to shift to other mandated academic programs or curriculum (e.g., Will they need to remove something from their curriculum?) When the leadership is aware that curriculum changes will not be necessary, it is one of the first things we should be able to communicate back to our teachers. Leaders hold space by promoting dialogue that lets all individuals participate in making decisions and adapting to new challenges together.

Minding Your Mood

Your mood matters to those you lead, especially during difficult times. Research on leadership development teaches us that our limbic system (the part of the brain involved in our emotional responses) has an open-loop design that lets other people change our emotions (Goleman, 2014). When we first interact with others, our bodies operate at different rhythms. However, after 15 minutes, our physiological profiles look remarkably similar. Researchers have seen again and again that emotions align in this way whenever people are near one another. As far back as 1980, psychologists Howard Friedman and Ronald Riggio found that even nonverbal expressiveness can affect other people (Friedman et al., 1980). For example, when three strangers sit facing one another in silence for a minute or two, the most emotionally expressive of the three transmits their mood to the other two without a single word being spoken.

The same holds true in our schools—we "catch" feelings from one another. Moods that start at the top tend to spread the fastest because everyone is watching the leaders. Research shows that an alarming number of leaders do not really know if they have resonance with their school culture (Walker, 2012). Some school leaders don't believe their emotions, attitudes, or mood can have an influence on the entire community. Whether they know it or not, they do: Moods, feelings, and states of mind are highly contagious throughout organizations (Goleman, 2014). Everyone in a school or district can be influenced by the leader's mood, and it is easier to "catch" a mood of anxiety than one of calm and resolve.

Communicating Realistically

When challenges arise, leaders must respond promptly and energetically; teachers, students, and parents need to know that leaders recognize the seriousness of the situation and are committed to addressing it. They must immediately announce that they are making the crisis their absolute priority while explaining that they need time to finalize the best course of action.

Perhaps the most essential element of crisis leadership is clear and trustworthy communication. Research shows that best practices for crisis communication include transparency, honesty, and empathy (Coombs, 2021). Some leaders choose to delay or dilute bad news so as not to worry or demotivate staff. This approach can reflect the leaders' own discomfort or anxiety with the situation. Staff suffer most from uncertainty; they almost always prefer finality to continuously imagining worst-case scenarios.

At the same time, leaders must learn to balance *honest* communication and *open* communication. For example, we should never share sensitive information about individual staff or students or certain types of school data. The best approach is to provide only whatever information is necessary and ensure that it is as relevant and digestible as possible, such as by representing it visually.

All leaders must find the right cadence or rhythm for their communication efforts during difficult times, and providing regular weekly updates can help them to practice doing so. Even if recipients don't read these updates, they send the message that the leader understands the need to regularly provide them with information.

Conclusion

It would be foolish to think that good old-fashioned IQ, experience in the field, and operational skills are not vital to strong school leadership, but the recipe would not be complete without strong emotional intelligence. The dimensions of emotional intelligence used to be seen as "nice to haves" in business and school leadership, but today we know they are actually "need to haves." As leaders, we must remove the stigma from leading with emotional intelligence, model the five dimensions, talk about them with students and staff, and look within ourselves for ways to improve. Thankfully, emotional intelligence can be learned. The process may be challenging and time-consuming, but the benefits make it worth the effort.

Reader Reflection

1. Which dimension(s) of emotional intelligence do you find you engage with the most?
2. Which dimension(s) of emotional intelligence do you find yourself needing to improve upon?
3. How can you recognize emotional intelligence in yourself?
4. Do you praise others for having high emotional intelligence? How so?
5. How can you tell if someone has high emotional intelligence?

6. How do you teach others to recognize self-awareness?
7. Do you agree that a school leader's moods and behaviors drive the moods and behaviors of everyone else?
8. Can you think of an example of a way your mood has affected the success of a program or strategy that you've implemented?
9. Can you recall a time when you had to "hold space" for your team? If so, were you successful?
10. How does (or should) empathy manifest itself in your communication style?
11. How does (or should) empathy manifest itself in your social skills?

2

Emotions and the Clarity of Your Vision During Difficult Times

When I ask a group of teachers, "What makes a good school leader?" I seldom have to wait long before someone says, "vision." Effective school leaders have a vision that inspires and moves people, providing them with direction and hope. Conversely, those without a vision can't really call themselves leaders. Too often, leaders fail to develop and work toward a clear vision of where their organization should be.

As a young school leader, I had a vision to help teachers create an environment that encouraged them to flow in and out of one another's classrooms to see their peers in action and learn best practices. To achieve this goal, I helped organize an instructional leadership team (ILT). The ILT met after school a couple times per month to discuss our instructional practices and our students' academic progress. At all our meetings, everyone was cordial and polite and we had some nice interactions and discussions. I thought things were going well, and I assumed that my vision for creating a school culture where teachers openly shared their instructional practices was coming to fruition.

I was wrong.

Eventually, I learned that teachers on the team were just humoring me; they were not actually going into one another's classrooms to capture best practices. They even joked that *ILT* stood for "Ignacio Lopez Talks." To remedy this situation, I had to let go of wanting total control of these meetings. I also realized I needed to be much clearer in communicating the vision and reasons for getting into one another's classrooms. Although I wanted teachers to follow my goals, they couldn't just be mine. We needed to develop—as a team—shared goals for this work. I couldn't have come to these realizations without self-awareness.

As this example shows, our emotional intelligence—particularly the dimensions of self-awareness, self-management, and empathy—can affect how we construct and communicate our organizational vision. In this example, I was leading teams with a vision to create open learning spaces, yet I was not clear enough about my objectives and did not trust teachers to help lead team meetings.

School leaders navigating difficult situations or implementing new processes often get frustrated with their teachers, thinking they "just aren't getting it." Much of the time, however, the fault lies not with the teachers but with the leader's unclear articulation of their vision.

Mission Versus Vision

When helping school leaders and staff develop a clear vision for their organizations, I inevitably get asked about the difference between a mission and a vision. A mission provides day-to-day clarity by defining the identity and scope of an organization. Without a clear mission, we can easily drift off target.

A mission statement answers three questions:
1. Who are we?
2. Who do we serve?
3. What do we deliver?

Even though these questions are important and necessary, they are not as important as a vision when navigating difficult times. It is a clearly communicated vision that will propel your students, teachers, and community to surmount challenges. (See Figure 2.1 for a further breakdown of the differences between mission and vision.)

Whereas a mission statement is like a tagline or bumper sticker message, a vision statement is a more robust document that describes the future you envision for your school and the children you serve. Preparing a vision statement requires you to sit and do some hard thinking.

When developing a vision statement, I recommend thinking three to five years out. Some leaders go a decade out, but in my experience, leaders tend to see the biggest gains over a three- to five-year period. If you are in the middle of navigating some sort of crisis, people want to feel as though you are managing the situation

FIGURE 2.1

Mission Statements Versus Vision Statements

	Mission Statements	**Vision Statements**
Area of Focus	The here and now	The future
Purpose	Answers the question "Who are our students and what are their needs?"	Answers the question "Where will we take our students and why?"
Features to Communicate	The organization's purpose and values; our responsibilities to our students, teachers, and communities	A brighter future for our students aligned with our values and culture

while keeping an eye on the future. Key aspects of your mission and vision can be gleaned from your school community's moods, stresses, and desires.

Let's say, as principal of a high school, you notice that there is a growing sense of stress and anxiety among students due to increasing academic pressure and competition. Additionally, you observe that many students are actively participating in environmental clubs and initiatives, showing a strong desire to make their school community more sustainable. Key aspects of your mission and vision in this situation could be

1. **Promote student well-being.** Based on the moods and stresses evident in the school community, one of the key aspects of your mission and vision would be to prioritize student well-being and mental health. You could implement programs to reduce academic pressures, provide additional counseling services, and foster a supportive inclusive environment.

2. **Strive for environmental sustainability.** Considering the students' desires to contribute to environmental causes, your mission and vision may include a focus on environmental sustainability. You can integrate eco-friendly practices into the school's curriculum and facilities.

3. **Increase community engagement.** Recognizing the importance of your students wanting to make an impact on the school community, your mission and vision may include fostering a strong sense of community engagement. This could involve encouraging open communication among students from different grade levels in your building about the environment. It could also mean involving parents and local stakeholders in decision-making processes around environmental sustainability.

The Four Focus Areas of an Effective Vision

Many leaders have difficulty looking three to five years into the future because they are so caught up in the here and now. The trick is not to overthink your vision. When you look into the future, don't look at the whole picture all at once. Emotionally intelligent school leaders know how to compartmentalize their vision planning. To ensure a successful vision, leaders should focus on the following four areas:

1. The future of your teachers and teams.
2. School programs.
3. Communication inside and outside your school(s).
4. The impact of your vision on others in the school community.

I recognize that some educators will want to reflect on additional variables as they plan. When I work with school leaders, we sometimes discuss issues such as community engagement, donor relationships (for private schools), school finances, labor agreements, and public relations. Still, the four variables listed here can take you pretty far.

The Future of Your School's Teachers and Teams

You can't propose a bold new future for students and families if you don't have a vision in place for your teachers and teacher teams. The right teams will help execute strategy, take care of students, and champion the cultivation of a welcoming school environment.

To ensure your vision includes teachers and teacher teams, consider these questions:

1. When you imagine your teachers three years out, where do you see them in terms of their talent, experience, and work-life balance?
2. What does your ideal teacher team look and sound like to you?
3. How does your school take care of teachers and cultivate a successful culture?

There are no right or wrong answers to these questions. Emotionally intelligent leaders want the best for their teachers; they should be deliberate in communicating those feelings. Faculty and staff should hear you articulate what it is you want for them now and in the future. Here, for example, are some of the things I've heard emotionally intelligent school leaders say repeatedly about the talent in their buildings during turbulent times:

- "Our faculty live and breathe our school's core ideology, and our teachers possess impeccable character and extraordinary talent, caring for all children and boasting a track record of success with children."
- "Our teachers experience reasonable autonomy, planning and executing their own work without the impediment of overbearing administration, ridiculous bureaucracy, or red tape."
- "We encourage innovation and experimentation. If something doesn't work, our teachers learn from it and move on."

Emotionally intelligent leaders reflect on their workforce and the impact that any crises or tough times may be having on them. Our talent should never be excluded from our vision planning, communication, or reflection.

School Programs

Vision planning and communication must address current and future school programs (both academic and nonacademic). A good way to start is by reflecting on questions such as these:

- What academic programs do we offer our students, parents, and community members?
- Do we offer academic programs that enable *all* learners to achieve success?
- Are our programs welcoming of *all* children and *all* families?

Remember, vision is about what comes next, not what's happening now; it's about where your school is guiding students. What's next for the academic programs in your school or district should be constantly on your mind. Ask yourself what programs you can create that will help fulfill your mission and create safer, more just, and more academically rigorous conditions for students.

I am reminded of a school district that was navigating issues of hate speech online and in its schools. Students flooded the school board meetings demanding action. The superintendent worked with the lead curriculum administrator and a group of students to propose a mandatory new anti-hate speech unit in the 9th grade history curriculum. The goal was for no one to graduate from the district without learning about the harms of hate speech.

This new program embedded in the curriculum wasn't the be-all and end-all, but it was a start, and it showed the community that the district could use programming to make a difference. This is a good example of how socially aware and empathetic leaders can leverage their position to improve conditions for teachers, students, and families.

Communication Inside and Outside Your School or District

It may seem intuitive, but you'd be surprised how often leaders forget to think deliberately about their communication plans and structures. It's pointless to talk about the future if nobody hears you. Too many leaders think that just because they put information out there, everyone knows about it, when in reality they've left most people completely in the dark. Emotionally intelligent leaders worry about being heard and understood.

When vision planning, think strategically about how to communicate messages both inside and outside your school. Communication is fundamentally about how you relate to staff, students, and community members. Emotionally intelligent leaders communicate their communication style. They do this often while addressing a room of faculty or parents or in an email communication. Here, for example, is how one school leader I know did this:

> I lead with transparency, and we will be a school that communicates clearly. My communications to you as a school community will come out once a month via email at the very least. I will use Facebook for messages pertaining to school activities weekly or as best I can. In the event of an emergency, we will institute the text messaging system, so please be sure you have signed up to receive text messages from me.

Clarity of communication and use of various channels are key to avoiding confusion and ensuring that everyone receives the messages you send.

The Impact of Your Vision on Others in the School Community

Emotionally intelligent leaders measure their progress; a vision doesn't mean much without some sort of metric in place to know whether and when it is achieved (e.g., "100 percent of our students will graduate having taking the district's anti-hate speech course."). Ask yourself: What will be the result of realizing our vision? This question can be answered in many ways. Most school leaders go right to the impact on students; others talk about the impact on their neighborhood or community. The only wrong answer is no answer at all. Here is one example: "We will have transformed the lives of *all* community members who pass through our doors and achieving outstanding results for the children we serve—and we will do it without compromising our values."

Assessing the Clarity of Your Vision

A vision should provide clarity in the midst of fogginess and uncertainty. Leaders tend to be somewhat abstract when first developing their vision statements. They are not only attempting to describe the unseen or the "not yet here" but also navigating their own emotions—and, in times of crisis, the immediate challenges they face. Michael Hyatt (2020) talks about the "curse of knowledge" when it comes to vision: The vision is obvious to us because we know what it is, so we assume everyone else knows it, too.

Have you ever wondered why your teachers or teams have scrambled to gain a full picture of the vision you are trying to communicate? Could it be that you have only given them a rough idea of where you'd like to see the school be in the next three to five years? Is the blueprint for your vision only in your head? Too often, leaders use generic phrases or buzzwords that can distract from what they're trying to get across.

In his research on the vision-driven leader, Hyatt (2020) found that a leader's visions tend to fall into one of four categories: vague, confusing, intuitive, or clear. Your words have the creative power to really move and energize teams, but they can also deflate those teams and sow confusion. To avoid the latter, work to ensure that your communication is not vague, confusing, or intuitive.

A Vague Vision

A vague vision can be categorized as more of a hunch or wishful thinking than an actual vision of where the school should be. When the picture in our own mind is not fully set, we fumble for the right words to use to communicate it and land on unhelpfully vague language. Teams end up wondering what is going on—or worse, they begin to fill in the gaps in ways that move us further from rather than closer to our goals.

I once worked with a school leader who was attempting to garner buy-in from parents and community members who were pushing back on consolidation of schools in the district. "By creating value for our students, we create value for you as parents," this leader said. "We will use our education expertise to create new programs and safe passageways for your children. Our teachers are energetic and respectful—they care about all your children." One of the parents answered back, "What are you talking about? We want you not to close *this* school, not to tell us about the value of another school!"

In this example, the leader failed to communicate or define the value or purpose of the consolidation plan while also failing to address the community's main concern: the closing of their school. This leader was communicating vaguely and didn't come across as empathetic or socially aware.

A Confusing Vision

Sometimes leaders are enthusiastic and energetic but unable to translate their positive emotions into the correct language to motivate their team. For example, you'll hear leaders talk about "creating synergies" between programs, taking the school to "another level," "picking the low-hanging fruit," or "creating disruption"—what do these things really mean? Use clear language to make sure you aren't confusing your team.

An Intuitive Vision

Some school leaders wrongly assume that their vision is obvious and should speak for itself. In my experience, this is never the case. We must be explicit about what we mean so our message registers correctly with faculty and staff. It took me some time to learn how important this is. Early on, I would lead with so much passion and conversation that I assumed everyone was intuitively on the same page with the school's vision and direction—after all, no one was asking questions or pushing back. I soon learned not to be complacent about this. At leadership team meetings, I would ask the team, "Be honest with me: Do we think our teachers and staff are really getting it?" I would challenge team members to paint the picture for me. Hearing back from my team members helped me to know if they were getting it and assured me that they'd be moving the same message forward.

Repetition and Pace

I have learned the importance of needing to repeat my vision to ensure it's been understood. If you don't like to repeat yourself, don't become a leader, as leaders will inevitably repeat their messages several times a day—and effective ones will use their self-awareness and self-management skills to endure the repetitive nature of this work.

School leaders help set the beat or rhythm for their school or district through their scheduling choices as well as through quick huddles in the hallway, one-on-one check-ins, annual reports, committee meetings, and so on. More recently, however, digital tools such as Slack, Teams, and Zoom have disrupted the conventional pace of work in schools. Our hyperconnectedness means teachers and teams often lack the moments of silence necessary to process, understand, and plan. Leaders therefore need to be more intentional about providing this time, encouraging teachers to disconnect, and deliberately scheduling quiet moments for processing information. Remember that, as a leader, you are in control of creating these moments for your staff.

Some school leaders preplan their emails or social media communications and use email tools that send out their prepopulated messages. They use forms and templates so that anyone on their team can complete the messages if they need to. These communications then go out automatically every Friday or once a month. depending on their urgency (Dixon, 2012). Following are some other strategies for addressing the pace of your communications:

- **Principal's corner.** Some school leaders keep an updated bulletin board in their school sharing images and information about the school's vision and progress toward goals.
- **Mini town hall meetings.** These meetings are communicated early in the year and are used to reiterate the vision and discuss whether the school or district is on track to see it come to fruition. These events can be great listening sessions for leaders, staff, and the community.
- **Themed engagement events on or off campus.** I am a fan of themed events. We are social beings who need to interact and connect with one another. To meet these needs

in the aftermath of the COVID-19 pandemic, I used to hold what I called "Tuesdays Together." One Tuesday a month, I invited teachers and staff to an optional, afterschool event with food, guest speakers, and conversation. We even started to record these sessions and offered participants the chance to join in via Zoom. These sessions lasted until groups began to form organically and folks started socializing on their own again.
- **Protocols for professional learning.** One great way to help teachers sit in process and dialogue is to design and use protocols to guide discussions and engagement. When team meetings are all about one person talking, people lose interest. Protocols for professional learning ensure that all team members have a voice at the table; they also ensure that we are capturing or documenting key ideas, charts, or visual aids accurately. (See Lois Brown Easton's 2009 ASCD book *Protocols for Professional Learning* for strategies to help your teams process information together.)

Conclusion

In writing this chapter, I am reminded of the phrase *principle over passion*. So many times, I have worked with leaders whose passion for leading change obscures their ability to clearly communicate a vision. Having "passion" for your work isn't wrong, but if you are a leader who is constantly discussing revolutionary ideas or cutting-edge technologies for your school and students without a cohesive and understandable vision or plan to get there, then you are at risk of seeing your passion lead you from one ambition to another without results.

Although your passion is what motivates you to succeed and to see all your students succeed, it is your message that will allow you to arrive at practical, tangible, relatable, measurable, and accountable action. When passion creeps into our vision statements a little too much, we end up overstating and overcommunicating, which can lead to confusion. As a result, faculty and staff are left feeling excited but uncertain about their specific roles in the larger picture. In my experience, the best way for leaders to control their passion is to surround themselves with the best team members and partners possible.

 Reader Reflection

1. Share the vision that you have for your organization with a colleague or friend. What is their reaction? Can they tell you whether your vision is clear?
2. What tips would you offer school leaders on writing an effective mission or vision statement?
3. Do any members of your leadership team think about vision in a way that contradicts the information in this chapter?
4. What vision do you have for the talent in your school(s)?
5. What results or value do the programs in your school or district deliver?
6. Whom do your programs help?
7. What does the program creation process look like in your school(s)?
8. How do you choose what new programming to offer students?

9. What makes your learning programs different than those in other schools or districts?
10. How do you plan to communicate effectively both inside and outside your school(s)?
11. What communication channels will best help deliver the messages you need to get out?
12. How big is your reach? How many families do you serve? How do you reach every single family?
13. Which of the following metrics are most meaningful to you?
    ___Student learning
    ___Student retention and graduation rates
    ___Diversity
    ___Faculty/teacher count and retention rate
    ___Program impact
    ___Organizational culture
    ___Budgeting and finance
14. How does your community think about your school or district? How do other communities and neighborhoods outside your boundaries think of your school or district? How have you collected these data?
15. Over the last month, how many times have you communicated your vision for your school(s)?
16. Can a colleague tell you how often you communicate your vision?
17. Are you the only one communicating a vision for your school or district?
18. Who helps you communicate your vision?

19. Do you use any signs or objects to help communicate your vision?
20. How would you define the saying "principle over passion"? What does this mean to you?
21. Do you agree that leaders should strike a balance between leading with principle and leading with passion? Why or why not?
22. What strategies have you used to "hear" yourself speak during meetings so you can catch yourself when you're being overly passionate in a situation that requires you to be more straightforward?

3

Creating and Leading Emotionally Intelligent Teams

The success of our schools, especially in difficult times, requires a team effort. Research shows that strong collaborative teams have an impact on both school culture and student success (Garet et al., 2016; Ronfeldt et al., 2015; Vescio et al., 2008). This chapter defines the characteristics of effective school teams and lays out the important connection between a leader's emotional intelligence and the emotional intelligence of teams. Far too often, we view emotional intelligence as an individual pursuit and fail to apply its dimensions to groups. Leaders must learn how to "incubate" teams or groups not only to help navigate difficult times but also to support the school culture and enhance student experiences.

Research by Druskat and Wolff (2001) shows both that the most effective teams are emotionally intelligent and that any team can attain emotional intelligence. What's more, the work of leading effective teams takes a great deal of emotional intelligence on the part of leaders. Successful team leaders are consultative and supportive; as expert persuaders, they manifest the dimensions of self-awareness, self-regulation, and empathy. These leaders know when to make an emotional plea to their teams, especially when an appeal to reason will not work, and recognize the need to ignite passion within teachers and staff.

The Characteristics of Effective School Teams

In my experience, the most effective emotionally intelligent teams share the following 10 characteristics:

1. Goals and values are clearly understood and accepted by everyone.
2. Teachers and community members are oriented toward meeting goals and achieving results.
3. Team members understand their assignments and the way their roles contribute to the work as a whole.
4. The basic climate is one of trust and support among team members.
5. Communications are open; teachers are willing and have opportunities to share all data relevant to team goals.
6. Teachers and staff are allowed to participate in making informed, evidence-based decisions.
7. All team members are involved in implementing decisions.
8. Leaders demonstrate strong support for all team members while maintaining high performance standards.
9. Differences are acknowledged and effectively addressed, rather than being overlooked or dismissed as superficial.
10. The team's structure, procedures, and membership align with completing the tasks and objectives.

Research on group emotional intelligence by Druskat and Wolff (2001) suggests that the following three conditions are also essential to a group's effectiveness:

1. There is a sense of trust among the members.
2. There is a shared sense of group identity among the members, creating a feeling of belonging and value.
3. There is a collective sense of group efficacy where team members believe in their ability to perform effectively as a group and recognize that working together yields better results than individual work.

In groups without these conditions present, team members tend to hold back rather than be fully engaged.

Key Norms of Emotionally Intelligent Groups

Leaders of effective teams create emotionally intelligent norms for team members to follow. These norms can eventually become a part of the school or district's culture. Group emotional intelligence is about bringing emotions deliberately to the surface during meetings and understanding how they affect the team's work. Group emotional intelligence involves not only fostering positive relationships within and outside the team but also leveraging emotions to strengthen the team's capacity to tackle challenges together. It involves exploring and embracing emotions in collaborative and honest ways.

Emotionally intelligent members do not necessarily make for an emotionally intelligent group. Leaders must be intentional and mindful of creating norms that reinforce trust, group identity, and group efficacy. In turn, these norms can help build the emotional capacity of all members, turning the team into a space where all members have the ability to respond constructively in emotionally uncomfortable situations and influence emotions in a constructive way. There are four types of group norms that help create such an environment: interpersonal understanding norms, perspective-taking norms, confrontation norms, and caring norms.

Interpersonal Understanding Norms

Team emotional intelligence is more complicated than individual emotional intelligence because teams interact at more levels (Druskat & Wolff, 2001). The self-awareness and self-regulation of individuals is directed first inward to oneself, then outward to others. A group, by contrast, must have an interpersonal understanding of its own emotions or moods (as a collective group) while also understanding the collective emotions of other groups in the school or district.

Emotional incompetence can cause teams to become dysfunctional. For example, consider the following scenario:

> Ms. K., head of her high school English department, is asked to join a new cross-functional team at her school to come up with ways of engaging students in the classroom. She has extensive experience and a real passion for student engagement, but her team members—seven teachers across various disciplines—find that she brings little more than a bad attitude to the table. At an early brainstorming session, Ms. K. sits silently with her arms crossed, rolling her eyes. When another teacher on the team starts to get excited about an idea, she launches into a detailed account of how a similar idea was tried in the past and failed. The group is confused; this is the student engagement star teacher that the principal was talking about? Little do they realize she feels insulted by the very formation of the team. To her, it implies that there is no student engagement occurring in the building and that she hasn't done her job of leading other groups focused on student engagement efforts.

In this scenario, an interpersonal understanding norm might help team members understand that Ms. K. is acting out of defensiveness. It is essential for the team to recognize this defensiveness in Ms. K if they want to communicate their intention of recognizing her past achievements rather than diminish them. Some effective interpersonal understanding norms include the following:

1. Hear from *all* members of the team, especially if starting a new initiative or voting on an issue.
2. Respect others' opinions and thoughts.
3. Don't take comments personally.
4. Include "venting" as an agenda item to round out meetings so folks can discuss what's on their minds.

Perspective-Taking Norms

Emotionally intelligent groups take the time to pause and hear out any objections before moving forward on a vote or plan of action. Even if there appears to be a consensus, such groups make sure to ask if everyone is completely behind the decision. Effective groups will also ask if there are any perspectives they have not heard yet or thought through completely. Team members should sit in silence or pause for a moment while others collect their thoughts (and, sometimes, their confidence) before speaking up. Some teams even add this time as an agenda item for meetings.

Confrontation Norms

Leaders can help regulate team members' emotions by establishing norms around confrontation. Teams must learn how to feel comfortable calling out members when they cross a line. When done right, with respect, and with emotional intelligence, such confrontation can be seen in a positive light. Some effective guidelines related to confrontation include the following:

1. Speak to the team leader first before confronting a fellow team member.
2. Confront others in private and in person whenever possible.
3. Confront others as soon as possible rather than looking for the "right" time to do so.
4. Stick to the issue when confronting a team member; make the point and do not repeat it.
5. Avoid sarcasm, especially in email or text messages.

Caring Norms

In my experience, establishing norms that reinforce caring behavior is not hard to do if we focus on the little things. In addition to acknowledging things such as birthdays and weddings, the team should be alert to signs that members are upset or concerned. For instance, if a teacher arrives upset to a meeting because of traffic or some other issue, it's wise for the team leader to acknowledge the sacrifice the teacher made to be there and thank that person publicly in the meeting for understanding the importance of the team's work. A caring team attitude includes displaying positive regard, appreciation, and respect for team members through support, validation, and compassion. Some effective caring norms include the following:

1. Validate members' contributions to the team and let them know the team values them.
2. Listen to and respect differences of opinion.
3. Never demean or belittle team members' ideas.

Incubating Emotionally Intelligent Teams

Emotionally intelligent teams work to monitor, share, communicate, and take ownership of key tasks, strategies, and programs in schools. These teams develop an eye for improving the quality of overall instruction, academic and behavioral interventions, after-school programming, learning management systems, technology-infused learning opportunities, and more. School leaders tend to land on one of three strategies for making these improvements: acquiring new programs, investing more money into existing programs, and "incubating" a team with the task of finding an approach, an idea, or a solution. Incubating a team can be the hardest strategy to implement, but in my experience, it is often the right way to go.

Some may argue that incubating a team takes too long or that they don't have the right teachers in the building to take it on. These are just excuses. Incubating a team with an idea invites teachers to become part of the improvement process. Teams that feel as though the administration has their back are more likely to take ownership of a task or problem. Following are some strategies for effectively incubating emotionally intelligent teams.

High-Stakes Thinking

When a school principal in a large urban district noticed the long distances that families were traveling to receive wellness services, she incubated a team in her school with the idea of developing a school wellness center to serve the entire community. You can imagine some of the pushback she received from families concerned about the mental health services being offered in the school building—something they didn't really know about or understand.

Rather than listening to the complaints, the principal worked with district leaders to incubate a small team of six, including two teachers and staff members from the district and a local community organization. After one year and several community and board meetings, the school board voted unanimously to approve a school wellness center. In this example, the stakes of not having a wellness center in place were high, as children were routinely pulled out of school to travel far away for services. When incubating teams, leaders need to articulate the high stakes of a situation to emphasize the importance of finding a solution.

Controlled Disorganization

School leaders should avoid overorganizing the work of teams if they want them to have the freedom to attack problems as best they see fit. Giving up control can be tricky for some leaders, but it can lead to more effective teams. In the example of the wellness center, the team succeeded despite a bit of chaos and disorganization. Though they had set times to meet, they rarely followed their agenda; sometimes they would pick up the phone on the spot to call a medical clinic or community organizer for advice or direction. They organized their findings in several Google documents but sometimes inadvertently locked the principal out of the files, causing brief delays in communication. They talked a lot during their meetings, sometimes into the late hours of the evening. They randomly visited with families in the community, walking them from their homes to the school building to show how close the center would be. Teams need to find their own rhythms, and we as leaders should provide them with the independence they need to be daring and bold and creative.

Leadership from Within

Sometimes a team will arrive at a proposal that is not quite what the leader pictured when incubating it, and that's OK. Our role as leaders is to celebrate the team's achievements and help put in place the leadership for implementing the proposal (hopefully a member or members of the same team). You never know when a team member might emerge as a new leader. In the case of the wellness center example, one of the teachers on the team became the center's director. We should be proud of the work teams do while also being ready to move on to the next steps in the process.

Conclusion

Incubating teams to think up new ways of doing things can go against the grain of older and larger school districts, but it is vital work. It requires creativity, flexibility, collaboration, speed, and a leader who is highly emotionally intelligent. Creating the capacity to conceive, develop, and administer new school services is essential if schools are to thrive in an increasingly fast-moving and hyperconnected world. There is no excuse for schools not to organize teams for improving the learning space. Even organizations with little money can incubate teams that lead to the increased impact and reach of services (Humble et al., 2015).

A school principal working to improve race relations in his school once asked me, "Do we always need to build new teams to incubate a new idea, or can we use current teams and committees?" We can indeed find opportunities to incubate new ideas in existing teams as long as we put in place norms for emotionally intelligent group work.

In the next chapter, I share how one emotional intelligent school leader with a clear vision, an incubated idea, and an emotionally intelligent team was able to begin monitoring gaps in culturally relevant teaching to address the needs of students at a time of rising racial tensions in the community.

Reader Reflection

1. What additional characteristics of effective emotionally intelligent teams would you add to the ones shared in this chapter?
2. How do you assess the effectiveness of teams in your school or district? Is this a formal or informal process?
3. How does a school leader's emotional intelligence influence the success of school teams?
4. What are some examples of interpersonal understanding norms you have used with teams?
5. What are some examples of perspective-taking norms you have used with teams?
6. What are some examples of confrontation norms you have used with teams?
7. What are some examples of caring norms you have used with teams?
8. How would you define the process of incubating a teacher team?
9. Can you share an example of a successfully incubated team in your school? How did the team operate?
10. What factors beyond those discussed in this chapter should school leaders be mindful of when incubating a team?

4

Increasing the Emotional Intelligence of Your School Culture

As we navigate difficult situations, we must take care not to lose sight of our overall school culture. When a school culture is positive, teachers are expressing a shared vision, communication is up, spirits are high, and students are succeeding; when it is negative, retention is down, teachers are not collaborating, and student discipline rates are rising. Establishing and maintaining a positive school culture is essential because research shows that there is a strong correlation between culture and performance (Cameron & Quinn, 2011; Huffington et al., 2004).

A school culture is the product of the social interactions and relationships among teachers, staff, and students in schools. The strength of a school's culture hinges on the interactions among individuals within the organization (Cameron & Quinn, 2011). A robust culture is characterized by numerous interconnected and harmonious exchanges among all members of the school community. These exchanges foster a widespread and reinforced understanding of the school's distinctive culture and an understanding of the key elements for succeeding within that culture. Conversely, a weak school culture can emerge when interactions between teachers and staff are limited or scarce.

School values are reinforced when everyone is communicating them and abiding by them across grade levels, disciplines, and job functions. In a strong school culture, leaders communicate directly with everyone—teachers, staff, counselors, families, and so on. Weak communication is the fault of leadership and will lead to a weak culture. Implementing key culture-building messages proves challenging when only some teachers are hearing directly from the school leadership, if staff are continually excluded from meetings, or if we continually have faculty and staff members operating in isolation from others.

Five Key Strategies for Shaping an Emotionally Intelligent Culture

In working with school leaders navigating such vexing issues as union strikes, layoffs, and race relations, the following five key strategies emerged as particularly effective for ensuring an emotionally intelligent school culture:

Challenge fundamental beliefs and assumptions. "We can't reach them all." "We're never going to get through this." Negative comments such as these often go by unremarked but cannot be let alone. Leaders need to replace this thinking on the spot: "We *can* reach *all* children." "We *will* get through this." Leaders cannot be afraid to speak up; they need to rise above the noise to confront erroneous beliefs and assumptions head on. As an example, I have seen school leaders post the walls of the teachers' lounge with pictures of students and their families alongside MAP assessment data to show that *all* students in the school were making gains.

Establish meeting and engagement norms. How members act in our school community has an obvious impact on our school culture. As school leaders, we should put in place norms of engagement that focus not only on celebrating one another but also on (respectfully) holding one another accountable. In Chapter 3, I shared the importance of establishing team norms for interpersonal understanding, perspective-taking, confrontation, and caring; the same is true for organizations as a whole. Accountability is vital: If members of the community aren't following the norms, how we engage with or discipline them will have a profound impact on our school's culture.

Create opportunities for shared experiences. It is through shared experiences that our teachers and staff develop relationships, greater social awareness, and empathy toward one another. As leaders, we can help manage and control shared experiences such as back-to-school workshops, professional development opportunities, and end-of-year celebrations. We should also consider creating additional shared experiences throughout the year, such as visits to conferences, cultural organizations, or other schools in the district.

Shared experiences include the use of new technology. For example, I once read about a CEO of a company who purchased virtual reality (VR) goggles for every employee as a way of providing them with a shared experience. I'm not saying we should buy VR sets for all our teachers (though that would be cool), but I am suggesting providing everyone in your community with some sort of unique shared experience. Perhaps all your teachers receive Uno game cards and are challenged to use them in innovative ways throughout the next term. Be creative and solicit the input of team members if you are struggling to come up with an idea.

Display evidence of your school's culture. The signs and images that you display in and around your building are key to promoting a positive culture (not to mention vital for communication). In their research on school environments, OWP Architects and colleagues (2010) point to the impact that building space has on communication, learning, and culture. What your school feels like, sounds like, and looks like is important. Students and families who enter a school should be able to see and feel its culture. Welcoming, inviting images of students on the walls; lessons being studied on the bulletin boards; signs for events happening in and around the school—all of these help establish the culture for visitors. When guests enter the main office, how are they treated? I can't count the number of times I have heard families complain about main office personnel being unfriendly. A welcoming and inviting main office is the first sign to newcomers that the school culture is a positive one.

Create, monitor, and share the success of your values. Creating a culture that not only believes in the values it establishes but also enacts those values is essential to creating a positive culture. During difficult times, leaders can turn to their school's or district's values for direction. If those values are not aligned with the direction that we need to be headed in, then we can begin editing or rewriting some of our values together. School leaders often review their organizational values, but rarely do they monitor when and where those values are being enacted.

Why School Values Are Important

Three different kinds of values—the ones we have for ourselves as educators, the ones we teach our students, and the ones schools make for themselves—govern our actions in schools. As leaders, we should ensure that our values reflect the kind of society we all want to live in. It is important for school leaders to understand that they can, with the assistance of their teachers and staff, identify a set of common values and purposes that underpin the school curriculum and the work of the school.

Research by Huffington and colleagues (2004) and Haydon (2007) shows that setting values allows people in organizations to achieve more consensus on issues. Remember, a school's values are core beliefs that are meant to be held by every member of a community. When co-constructed by members of the school community, values can give educators focus and a greater sense of purpose and engagement. They are a foundational building block of the school's culture and a constant reference point, especially during difficult times.

Values Help Attract and Retain Talent

We live at a time when the education profession is suffering a great loss of teachers. The research suggests that teachers leaving the field isn't always about the money (though we should definitely pay teachers more) but because the culture is weak, camaraderie is lacking, and the administration is unsupportive (Ingersoll, 2001, 2003). A value system that reflects the energy teachers bring and supports their work can encourage your current teachers to stay in their roles. Additionally, having teachers co-construct, support, and live out your school's values can make them feel more connected to the school and to one another.

Values Support a Calibrated Mindset and Emotional Security

A set of defined values in schools gives teachers a code of sorts to follow that can guide their conduct, calibrate their mindset, and provide them with a strong sense of security. For example, confrontation norms such as those discussed in Chapter 3 can ensure that your school effectively identifies and deals with toxic behaviors. Administrators know what they can expect from teachers and staff, and teachers and staff know what they can expect from administrators—no surprises.

Case Study: Principal Ted

A few years ago, I received a phone call from Ted, a former doctoral student who had become a school principal in a nearby town. He explained to me some of the difficulties he had been experiencing with his faculty, staff, and parents who had divergent opinions about how we should be educating children. Principal Ted's elementary school, which had primarily served middle-class white students in the past, had recently seen its minority population grow to nearly 40 percent of the school's population. Math and reading data made it clear that minority students were being left behind.

Over the previous two years, Principal Ted had started purchasing new interventions for students and examining his teachers' instruction to find ways of creating relevancies between teachers and students. When an article in the local newspaper came out about minority students in the district being left behind, pressure mounted from the community, parents, and the mayor's office for school leaders to address the issue. Ted's school was the worst in the district in terms of serving minority students.

When Principal Ted called me on that early fall day, his voice was calm despite the furor around him. There was a peace about him, yet he knew he needed help. Ted's social awareness allowed him to understand what he needed: someone to come in and speak to a team he had incubated for the purpose of closing the minority achievement gap. He (and the teacher team) felt that an outside voice could help amplify the idea that *all* children can learn. And the outside voice he had in mind was me.

Principal Ted had been laying out a vision for the success of all students; closing the math and reading achievement gaps of his minority students; and promoting a welcoming culture of inclusivity, access, and innovation. Since arriving as a leader at the school, he had communicated his vision in a way that encouraged teachers to organize and deliberately attack the achievement gap problem.

In his own way, Principal Ted had begun to create a small community within the larger community of teachers who really wanted to actively be engaged in addressing minority achievement gap issues. The pressure of news coverage only inflamed their sense of urgency. Some teachers in the building began to recognize that certain colleagues didn't seem to care about the achievement gap or believed there was nothing they could really do about it. There were small pockets within the larger culture of teachers who felt that they could never reach all children. School leaders need to challenge these negative assumptions, and that is exactly what Principal Ted and his teacher leaders did.

Steps for Creating a Values-Aligned Culture

I accepted Principal Ted's offer to meet with his teacher team. Rather than begin by discussing the negative mindsets in the school, we focused on celebrating positive behaviors that were relevant to the school's mission and values. Following are the steps we took over the course of one academic year to address challenges in the school's culture. These action steps are a great guide to culture building in your school.

Step 1: As a team, read one or two articles focused on the issue at hand. Doing this introduces an outside voice to the group, allowing members to comment freely on what they read. Ted's team wanted to focus their efforts on culturally relevant teaching and student engagement, both issues aligned to Ted's vision for the school. To this end, they chose to read two texts: "Yes, But How Do We Do It? Practicing Culturally Relevant Pedagogy" by Gloria Ladson-Billings (2023) and Chapter 2 from Zaretta Hammond's 2014 book *Culturally Responsive Teaching and the Brain*. They didn't just read these pieces individually; they chose to host professional development days around them. The texts were placed in each teacher's mailbox with instructions to read them before the next professional development meeting. The team facilitated discussion of the texts, encouraging teachers to relate them to their own practices. These texts held a mirror back to teachers, challenging them to articulate their own thoughts and actions with respect to culture, safety, and the success of all children.

Step 2: Unpack students' academic success data. Following the readings and discussion about culturally relevant teaching, the team met to take a deep dive into their students' academic achievement data. Though these data had been shared many times with teachers, no one seemed to be taking them seriously. The data showed increasing disparities between Black and Hispanic students and their white counterparts. Over the previous three years, the school had seen 43 percent of Black and Hispanic students drop below the minimum standards requirements for both math and reading, with Black students going from 22 to 50 percent below standard and Hispanic students from 14 to 48 percent below standard. By comparison, white students had less than 5 percent of students performing below standards over the previous three years.

The team's goal was to leverage these data to recalibrate teachers' mindsets. Some teachers in the school believed they were already providing students with culturally relevant learning. If that was the case, then why were achievement gaps only getting worse? The team hosted a second professional development day for teachers where they broke the data down by race, making the extent of learning disparities clear.

Step 3: Examine educator behaviors relative to the data. Discussions of school data should turn to what we as educators must do to improve conditions for students. Team members should ask if the data show they are enacting school values in a way that supports every student's learning journey.

Step 4: Identify ways to assess progress. Ted's team reviewed some great research on cultural and linguistic competencies from Georgetown University, including a self-assessment checklist for teachers providing services and supports in early childhood settings (Goode, 2009). This turned out to be a fantastic tool that helped the team think through the cultural relevance of instruction in the school.

In one afternoon, the leadership team, Principal Ted, and I reviewed 49 competencies from the Georgetown University document (Goode, 2009), and we decided on the following seven that we wanted to see enacted throughout the school's classrooms:

1. "I display pictures, posters, and other materials that reflect the cultures and ethnic backgrounds of children served."

2. "I ensure that the book/literacy area in my classroom has pictures and storybooks that reflect the different cultures of children and families served in my classroom."

3. "I read a variety of books exposing children in my early

childhood program or setting to various life experiences of cultures and ethnic groups other than their own."

4. "I plan trips and community outings to places where children and their families can learn about their own cultural or ethnic history as well as the history of others."

5. "I select videos, films, or other media resources reflective of diverse cultures to share with children and families served in my classroom."

6. "I am cognizant of and ensure that curricula I use include traditional holidays celebrated by the majority culture as well as those holidays that are unique to the culturally diverse children and families served in my classroom."

7. "I encourage and invite parents and family members to volunteer and assist with activities in my classroom."

After reading through the competencies, the team created a tool with which to assess whether teachers' classroom practices were culturally relevant. This survey, shown in Figure 4.1, was used to measure how much teachers in the school valued the seven competencies the team had selected and how much they believed the competencies were being enacted in the school. Twenty-four teachers completed the survey on their own in Google Docs.

After compiling the survey results, the team was able to identify three competencies with especially large gaps between how often they were enacted and how valued they were by teachers. Rather than spend a ton of time focusing on all seven of these competencies, the team chose to focus on improving these three areas for the remainder of the school year. During a professional development day, the team unpacked the survey data with teachers and explored possible strategies for closing the gaps they'd identified.

FIGURE 4.1

Teacher Survey for Assessing the Value of Competencies

	Culturally Relevant Teaching Competencies	**Enacted**			
		1 Never	**2** Sometimes	**3** Usually	**4** Always
1	I display pictures, posters, and other materials that reflect the cultures and ethnic backgrounds of children served.	0.00% 0	25.00% 6	**58.33% 14**	16.67% 4
2	I ensure that the book/literacy area in my classroom has pictures and storybooks that reflect the different cultures of children and families served in my classroom.	4.16% 1	8.33% 2	41.66% 10	**45.83% 11**
3	I read a variety of books exposing children in my early childhood program or setting to various life experiences of cultures and ethnic groups other than their own.	0.00% 0	12.50% 3	29.17% 7	**58.33% 14**
4	I plan trips and community outings to places where children and their families can learn about their own cultural or ethnic history as well as the history of others.	16.67% 4	**62.50% 15**	12.50% 3	8.33% 2
5	I select videos, films, or other media resources reflective of diverse cultures to share with children and families served in my classroom.	4.16% 1	**45.83% 11**	41.66 10	8.33% 2
6	I am cognizant of and ensure that curricula I use include traditional holidays celebrated by the majority culture as well as those holidays that are unique to the culturally diverse children and families served in my classroom.	8.33% 2	8.33% 2	4.83% 11	37.50% 9
7	I encourage and invite parents and family members to volunteer and assist with activities in my classroom.	25.00% 6	**33.33% 8**	20.83% 5	20.83% 5

	Culturally Relevant Teaching Competencies	**Value/Importance**			
		4 Essential	**3** Usually Important	**2** Somewhat Important	**1** Unimportant
1	I display pictures, posters, and other materials that reflect the cultures and ethnic backgrounds of children served.	79.17% 19	20.83% 5	0.00% 0	0.00% 0
2	I ensure that the book/literacy area in my classroom has pictures and storybooks that reflect the different cultures of children and families served in my classroom.	91.67% 22	8.33% 2	0.00% 0	0.00% 0
3	I read a variety of books exposing children in my early childhood program or setting to various life experiences of cultures and ethnic groups other than their own.	100.00% 24	0.00% 0	0.00% 0	0.00% 0
4	I plan trips and community outings to places where children and their families can learn about their own cultural or ethnic history as well as the history of others.	54.17% 13	41.67% 10	4.17% 1	0.00% 0
5	I select videos, films, or other media resources reflective of diverse cultures to share with children and families served in my classroom.	54.17% 13	41.67% 10	4.17% 1	0.00% 0
6	I am cognizant of and ensure that curricula I use include traditional holidays celebrated by the majority culture as well as those holidays that are unique to the culturally diverse children and families served in my classroom.	79.17% 19	20.83% 5	0.00% 0	0.00% 0
7	I encourage and invite parents and family members to volunteer and assist with activities in my classroom.	50.00% 12	25.00% 6	25.00% 6	0.00% 0

Reaping the Rewards

As the school year progressed, the team was able to capture and share best practices with teachers across the school. They leveraged learning walks and instructional rounds to show culturally relevant teaching practices that aligned to each of three competencies they had identified. They also identified "demonstration classrooms" where new teachers could see strategies enacted that were aligned to the school's values. Principal Ted and the team embedded instructional leadership into their school's culture that focused on cultural responsive practices to ensure the learning of *all* students in their school. And the data showed their efforts to be a resounding success: Almost three years after the team began its work, only 22 percent of Black students and 18 percent of Hispanic students were performing below standard in math and reading.

Conclusion

Principal Ted had a clear vision: to create a welcoming environment for all and close the achievement gap between white and minority students. His emotional intelligence allowed him to recognize that he needed additional help to make his vision a reality, so he incubated a team of teachers to examine the school's values and establish a value system focused on culturally responsive teaching. Ted and his team were able to affect their school's culture by calibrating their thoughts on cultural responsiveness, identifying key competencies they believed were important to the success of all students, and monitoring both teacher and student data.

One thing I love about Principal Ted's approach is that it was completely unthreatening to teachers. No individual was punished or shamed; the emphasis was on the school culture as a whole. It was the data, not the principal or the team, that spoke the loudest.

Reader Reflection

1. Reflect on your school or district culture. How would you define it? How do you think your culture got that way?
2. How can the culture of your school(s) support or detract from navigating through difficult times?
3. How big a role does culture play in your leadership?
4. Has your school culture changed due to unforeseen circumstances? How so?
5. Which of the following areas are you most proficient in, and which might you want to learn more about? Can you provide examples of what these areas might look like in your practice or in the practice of other leaders with whom you have worked?
   ___Challenging fundamental beliefs and assumptions
   ___Establishing meeting and engagement norms
   ___Creating opportunities for shared experiences
   ___Displaying evidence of your school culture
   ___Creating, monitoring, and sharing the success of your values
6. What are some unique shared experiences among staff in your school or district?
7. Is there room to grow intentional shared experiences between your teams? How so?
8. How have you successfully challenged the erroneous beliefs of teachers and staff?

9. What other characteristics or practices would you argue are essential to shaping a successful school culture?
10. Which of the following strikes you as the highest priority in your school community?
    ___ Attracting and keeping talent
    ___ Communicating clearly
    ___ Creating emotional security for the community
11. What key practices might you want to see enacted in your school(s)?
12. What is your school or district's current value system?
13. Do your teachers enact your school's values? How do you know?
14. Are there key strategies or instructional practices that all your teachers value and enact? How might your school go about measuring the gap between what is valued versus what is enacted in the learning spaces?
15. If there were a key signature instructional strategy that you would want all teachers to implement, what would it be and why?

5

Emotional Intelligence and External Stakeholder Engagement

In the previous chapter, I described the need to monitor and grow a healthy school culture that sets the right values and moves toward supporting all students. This culture work continues in the involvement and engagement of stakeholders outside the school environment such as small businesses, faith-based organizations, elected officials, and more. Though leaders must communicate to these stakeholders that they are committed to their roles and intend to be here for the long haul, the truth is that relationships between schools and communities will outlast most school leaders. Nurturing relationships with external stakeholders is therefore pivotal to a successful school culture.

Stakeholder engagement is the process by which a school involves people who may be affected by decisions in the decision-making or implementation process (Epstein, 2019; Tran et al., 2019). Engagement is different from involvement; it is not merely about including individuals in social events, fundraising efforts, or volunteering opportunities. These are all important, but I am referring to collaboration focused specifically on educating students. In my experience, leaders setting the stage for successful external stakeholder engagement have the following four expectations in place for teachers and staff in their schools.

Be transparent about school data. Faculty and staff are expected to share information about assessment practices, grading scales, and so on as requested by external stakeholders. This also includes sharing of any other additional metrics pertaining to the school's strategic efforts. Stakeholders should receive sufficient data to participate actively with helping students learn. The information we share must be clear, accurate, and meaningful; we can't assume that all stakeholders speak the jargon of schools. Unpacking and coaching our families to learn how to ask the right questions about their students' learning is key. Teachers should be prepared to answer questions such as "What have you taught my child in the last two months?" or "In what academic area has my child grown the most?"

Focus on students. When designing external stakeholder engagement opportunities, make sure those opportunities are directly aligned with student learning or SEL goals.

Develop authentic partnerships. Efforts to engage external stakeholders must be collaborative and genuine. There are meaningful roles for each party to play, and these must be clearly articulated. At every event in which external stakeholders are invited, offer opportunities for further engagement or collaboration. You should want to hear from your stakeholder groups as much as they want to hear from you.

Be inclusive and welcoming. All teachers and staff should welcome and engage with *all* families, operating from common values and a common vision that *all* students can be successful.

Trends in Community–School Relationships

Studies by Topor and colleagues (2010), Tran and colleagues (2019), and Epstein (2019) show that the level of parent and community engagement plays a crucial role in determining how the school environment influences student achievement. Over the last 10 years, we have seen the rise of community-based organizations focused on supporting the engagement and involvement between parents and schools. In contrast to conventional parent involvement, parent and community organizing takes on the responsibility of holding schools accountable for their outcomes and actions, often resulting in policy, practice, and resource changes (Henderson & Mapp, 2002).

During difficult times, you are likely to encounter organized groups of parents and community members demanding transparency before all the facts are even clear. In these situations, school leaders must maintain a high level of emotional intelligence and decorum to model how they communicate and move toward collaborative resolutions. Too often, school leaders are dismissive of individuals who are not directly tied to the day-to-day operations of a school or district. They want to involve certain stakeholders as little as possible so they can focus on the important work of the school. Although this is understandable, it's a tension that school leaders with high emotional intelligence learn how to manage.

The Key Components of External Stakeholder Engagement

Having honest, frank conversations with external stakeholders may be difficult but will yield the insights you need to surmount whatever challenges you face. Ignoring external stakeholder groups will only bring deeper scrutiny, vocal criticism, and reputational damage. At the very least, school leaders need to understand the perspectives of stakeholders. Research on the topic suggests that there are six key components of external stakeholder engagement (Detert et al., 2001; Epstein, 2019; Tran et al., 2019):

1. Knowing how to identify external stakeholder groups.
2. Repeating the organization's vision and seeking out context.
3. Strengthening communication among stakeholder groups.
4. Codesigning protocols of engagement with external stakeholder groups.
5. Following through on commitments.
6. Encouraging stakeholder ownership.

Knowing How to Identify External Stakeholder Groups

Not every stakeholder group is going to be the same, so it's a good idea to map the groups out and think strategically about the issues you want them to engage with. One way to identify stakeholder groups is by breaking them into the following five categories:

1. **Obligation:** Individuals or entities (groups, partners, or vendors) who currently have or might have agreements or contracts with the school, obligating them to fulfill a specific set of goals, responsibilities, or programs for the benefit of the school or students.
2. **Influence:** Individuals (or influencers) who are currently or potentially in a position to influence the ability of your school, or individuals within your school, to achieve established goals. Their affiliations or actions are likely to support or hinder the school's performance.

3. **Proximity:** Individuals with whom your school engages the most, encompassing internal stakeholders, families with longstanding connections to the school or community, and those residing in the immediate school boundaries.
4. **Reliance:** Individuals who have the most reliance include your teachers and staff, students, families, and all others who depend on the school for their own well-being and success.
5. **Representation:** Individuals who have the responsibility to advocate for and represent others, such as heads of local community organizations, union leadership, elected officials, or leaders of faith-based organizations.

Repeating the Organization's Vision and Seeking Out Context

As school leaders, we need to be telling, retelling, and further reiterating our vision with both internal and external stakeholders. As an old saying reminds us, leading is repeating. It is also important to take into account any information that may have been communicated to these groups in the past. Particularly if you are new to your role, you'll need to know if your predecessor engaged these groups and, if so, if there was any follow-through. Emotionally intelligent leaders seek out context. Learn about stakeholder groups by asking colleagues about them or attending off-campus events with them.

Strengthening Communication Among Stakeholder Groups

Emotionally intelligent leaders make good-faith efforts to strengthen the lines of communication among stakeholder groups.

Leaders can help the stakeholders think about their pattern and pace of communication with one another and encourage them to create their own communication channels in collaboration with a school or district leadership team. We want stakeholders to know they have the option to engage with us through multiple channels.

Codesigning Protocols of Engagement with External Stakeholder Groups

Emotionally intelligent leaders work with external groups to develop protocols of engagement. Here are some examples:

- Make involvement voluntary rather than mandatory.
- Invite full participation. Be mindful of groups that don't attend meetings and make it a point to strengthen their participation.
- Embrace the process and be flexible. Yes, you will get off track. Yes, meetings will sometimes start late or run over.
- Build trust with and among stakeholders.
- Stakeholders might not do things the way you'd like them to, but if they are moving in the right direction, let them arrive at a solution in their own way.
- Process and reflect on this work with leadership team members, teachers, and staff. Don't be negative about what's not working; think positively about the direction you are heading in or *could be* heading in.

Following Through on Commitments

Leaders need to think deliberately about how they follow up and follow through on their commitments. There is nothing more frustrating to external stakeholders than not getting any follow-up after a meeting or discussion with the school leadership. Never leave stakeholder meetings without a plan in place for next steps and follow-up. Clearly review priorities, meeting dates, and deadlines for action items. At the start of meetings, show stakeholder groups the work that has been done since the last meeting. I have also seen leaders kick off their meetings with a review of the last meeting's action items. Members should be honest about what has and hasn't been completed.

Encouraging Stakeholder Ownership

People support what they feel a sense of ownership over. I've heard it said that no one washes their rental car. A sense of ownership helps create a personal connection to the school and inspires stakeholders to contribute. It strengthens people's confidence and builds internal capacity as stakeholders increase their knowledge of the school and learn by seeing directly what works and what doesn't.

Case Study: Wilson High School

As a young educator working in the Chicago Public Schools, I was proudly involved with several community-based initiatives that focused on educating parents and communities about their children's education. I used to lead parent involvement and parent engagement professional development sessions for schools across the district. The focus of my presentations was on the effect that family engagement had on the overall success of children. I worked in the high school during the day and spent certain evenings delivering professional development at schools across the city.

In the spring of 2013, an article came out announcing the closure of 50 schools across the city (Riddell, 2013). A parent brought the article to one of my evening sessions and asked, "Why are they doing this? What does this mean for our children?"

I remember not having the right words at the time to speak to the changes happening across the city. I remember the article talked about low-performing schools that parents referred to as "dropout factories." Just a few years earlier, *Education Week* had found that 35 high schools across Chicago were deemed "dropout factories" (Alexander, 2007; Balfanz & Legters, 2006). Parents had started to use the same language with confusion and worry.

Shortly after the school closures were officially announced, more than 50 schools and community groups mobilized to save some of the buildings in their neighborhoods. I was invited to participate in a roundtable of community leaders addressing the closures and the impact they would have on local communities. I remember feeling underprepared and overwhelmed at that meeting in front of hundreds of people demanding answers. I wasn't the guy closing the schools, I was the guy trying to help the community make sense of the situation and provide strategies to navigate it.

I walked out of that meeting discouraged and confused. I learned at that moment that our community stakeholders—from parents to community leaders to faith-based organizations—all brought their own unique convictions and perspectives on the closures to the table. This is where the emotional intelligence of school leaders comes in. Some leaders at the roundtable spoke to a set of metrics that parents and community members weren't interested in (e.g., decreased enrollment, upkeep costs). It felt as though school leaders were simply telling the community about changes that were being imposed upon them rather than in collaboration with them.

Reflecting on my way home from the roundtable, I realized it was a missed opportunity to find common ground with our community stakeholders. Though there was no way, in a place as big as Chicago, to address every community being affected by closures, we could at least try to work closely with one or two communities.

One of the high schools slated for closure, Wilson High, had a rich history in the city, so the community roundtable decided to focus its efforts on saving it. With help from the mayor and other city officials, we were able to save the building by making it a turnaround school. The community was pleased that the school had been saved, but they were confused about what this turnaround entailed. No one in the community really knew what *turnaround* meant.

To help educate the community about turnaround schools, I spoke at a few local events but not before meeting with the school principal and administration to calibrate our language and establish supports. The newly appointed principal of the school, Ms. April, was awesome. She recognized the school's long history in the community. As this turnaround school received new teachers and new administrators, the school, students, and community remained the same. The building received upgrades and a new football field. The soul of the school and the community remained.

Although the community could easily understand the value of improvements to the building, they were more skeptical about changes related to instruction and assessment. The roundtable and school administration did not shy away from discussing these issues with the community. I helped them design three family and community engagement events focused on the school's approaches to teaching and learning in a way that was clear and understandable. This way, when they interacted with the school, they would know the right questions to ask. The sessions went really well. It helped that they were held at a local church near the school.

Involvement was voluntary, and we advertised the meetings after Sunday church services around the community.

Building trust with stakeholders takes a ton of patience. The work doesn't move fast, the communication and organizing takes time, and even when things are planned and meetings are scheduled, there will inevitably be changes or disruptions. Though our meetings ran late and we got off topic several times, the end results were great.

Stakeholder engagement can and will be messy, so our emotional intelligence instincts need to be on high alert. What we sound like, what we look like, how we dress: All of these things can make a difference one way or another. At the end of the day, this work isn't about you the school leader but about the children we serve. I think many school leaders get the stakeholder engagement thing wrong by making it about themselves and their leadership style. Ms. April and I saw the success of our stakeholder engagement efforts when parents at the school's first open house night asked questions such as "How much has my child grown on the MAP assessment?" and "You have had my child in class since September. What has she learned in that time?"

Conclusion

The research tells us that parent and community involvement will only continue to increase in our schools (Epstein, 2019; Tran et al., 2019). The success of such involvement will depend on whether leaders have the stamina, organizational structure, and emotional intelligence to communicate clearly and effectively while keeping their focus on what matters most: the education of students.

Reader Reflection

1. What expectations do you have for your teachers and staff about engaging with external stakeholders?
2. Can internal school culture affect how we think about external stakeholder engagement? How so?
3. What are some examples of how you communicate your expectations to your internal teams about external engagement?
4. Describe or define any expectation you would add to those discussed in this chapter and explain why you think they are important.
5. Describe the community engagement and relationship trends in your school over the last five years. Are there trends you are picking up on that will impact how you plan to engage stakeholders this year?
6. How would you define your current school's stakeholder groups? Can you identify them?
7. What are examples of ways you might get external stakeholder groups to dialogue with one another?
8. What engagement protocols do you have in place collaborating with external groups?
9. How do you ensure that you will follow through on your commitments with external stakeholder groups?
10. Discuss the concept of ownership and how it develops with a colleague.
11. What would you argue is the biggest challenge leaders face related to external stakeholders?

12. Why do you think some school leaders fail to effectively engage external stakeholders?
13. How did Wilson High School begin planning for stakeholder engagement? What common ground did district administrators and the community share?
14. What makes Ms. April an emotionally intelligent leader?
15. If you were in the same situation as Ms. April, what additional information would you need to further engage external stakeholders?
16. How did Wilson High School measure its success with external stakeholders?

6

Navigating Naysayers and Resisters During Difficult Times

During difficult times, we often see a rise in resisters and naysayers. In my experience, this is usually rooted in a fear of the unknown, which can cause people to say things they don't necessarily mean or fully comprehend (Carleton, 2016). During the COVID-19 pandemic, for instance, we saw the rise of community leaders and parents attending school board meetings to denounce masking and at-home learning protocols.

In his 2008 book *So Much Reform, So Little Change*, Charles Payne argues that countless reform efforts have failed largely due to a disconnect between schools and communities, especially in poor and stressed neighborhoods. There is no shortage of ideas for solving school problems: more teachers, smaller classes, later start times, more cultural training, less cultural training—the list goes on. Though I am sure each of us has opinions on any one of these issues, school leaders will never get total consensus on them. Placating all resisters and naysayers is a fool's errand; the best you can do is manage expectations and tensions while keeping your eye on the prize: the health and success of the children who pass through your school walls.

Interpreting Naysayers Correctly

The first step in navigating naysayers and resisters is understanding your own emotions and how you interpret the concerns of others. Not all resistance is bad, and how you receive dissent will affect how others receive it. Resisters and naysayers can cause a lot of confusion and noise in our school spaces. Students and teachers are looking to us as leaders for ways to respond. Our actions and inaction will have consequences.

Self-awareness is especially important when addressing dissent. We should take care not to automatically interpret a naysayer's words as an attack on us. Don't immediately go to negative thoughts such as "They want to see me out of this position" or "They're trying to knock me down." Rather, ask self-reflective questions such as "Is what I am being challenged on truly about our support for students?" and "Is there a way to reframe our approach so that it more clearly addresses student outcomes?"

Too often, leaders make up their minds about a naysayer's agenda without thinking of alternative possibilities. Be vulnerable with resisters—develop an emotional connection with them before assuming they are on the attack. Don't take hearsay from teachers or other administrators as truth; learn and understand resisters' stances for yourself before passing judgment. Remember that you have the power to adjust, expand on, pass along, or simply deny the requests of naysayers.

Using Emotional Intelligence to Engage Naysayers and Resisters

In just about every team I've worked with over the last 20 years there has been at least one naysayer or resister. And in almost every case, other team members were annoyed by that individual's behavior, finding them unhelpful and wishing for them to be removed or excluded. Some dissenting members were deliberately excluded from discussion, given the silent treatment, or even attacked—behaviors that are clearly unhealthy for an education learning environment.

It is obviously not easy working with difficult people. My challenge to leaders is to be mindful of your reactions when dealing with those who express dissent. Remember the importance of remaining empathetic in cases of conflict. Self-awareness is key. When everything is going smoothly and the flow is overwhelmingly positive, disagreement can feel especially unwelcome. Sometimes it can even feel as though the naysayer is intentionally derailing the conversation. Nevertheless, emotionally intelligent school leaders know not to place too high a value on harmony in every gathering, as making true progress on issues requires us to be honest and forthright with one another. Indeed, research shows that opposition can be beneficial to groups, making them more effective and productive (Argyris, 1990; Janis, 1972; Tversky & Kahneman, 2003). Criticism is necessary for innovation.

In her research on naysayers in organizations, Eileen Chou (2018) suggests there is a link between dissent and the endowment of power; by leveraging their agency, they can be perceived as strong and independent and rise to positions of leadership. We must have the emotional intelligence, confidence, and courage to engage with those who challenge us sooner rather than later.

Emotionally Intelligent Ways to Engage with Naysayers and Resisters

In my experience, the following practices have emerged as effective strategies for engaging with naysayers and resisters in ways that leverage the emotional intelligence of leaders.

Engage naysayers to bring about better outcomes. Emotionally intelligent school leaders recognize the impact that naysayers can have on a group or team. They may instinctively want to devalue the naysayers' voice, but socially aware leaders know when to include the opposition and when to dismiss it. They must be aware enough to know that including opposing perspectives while demonstrating empathy and compassion can lead them to solutions they might not have otherwise considered. Research suggests that solutions made by diverse groups with multiple perspectives are often better than those made by homogenous groups (Page, 2008; Phillips et al., 2006, 2014).

To engage effectively with naysayers, leaders must remain as aware and centered as possible and operate from their highest selves. This means avoiding distractions (put your cell phone down and look at the person) and actively listening. We should observe our own ego wanting to react negatively to the resistance in anger. Invite challengers to probe deeper: "Why are you worried that things won't work out in the end?" "What concerns do you have about being included or having a part to play on the team?" "Why do you think our plan going forward is not clear?" Emphasize the strength that resisters bring to the table, both to them and to other team members.

Be open and reflect on your emotions. Even if you are sure your stance is the right one, take the time to seriously consider and evaluate opposing ideas—and don't be afraid to be influenced. In my experience, people with opposing viewpoints almost never have bad intentions; they are usually advocating for something they believe is valuable.

When facing dissent, manage your emotions by taking a break to reset. It's perfectly OK to step out of the room for a few minutes. Name what you are feeling; have a conversation with yourself about your emotions. Are you feeling anger, sadness, disappointment, resentment, fear? Naming your emotion in the moment can help you more clearly share how you feel with the parties involved.

Seek to build relationships. Emotionally intelligent leaders look for paths to building relationships with resisters. Of course, not every relationship will be all rainbows and unicorns, but creating connections is vital to collaborative problem solving. One way to start building a relationship with naysayers is to give them feedback. Tell them that you see value in their different viewpoint and that you appreciate what they are contributing.

You can also suggest that naysayers share when they agree with you and the group so they are not seen as instinctual resisters (e.g., "I recognize that we may not always agree on decisions, but I appreciate when you acknowledge that we are on the same page.").

Communicate your self-awareness. Being transparent about your self-awareness can be difficult. Some leaders are afraid of sharing too much or appearing too vulnerable. However, being open about our emotions can lead us to recognize that we need to step back and view things from a systemwide rather than a personal perspective. In doing so, leaders demonstrate awareness, authenticity, and self-management. I have heard leaders say, "I think I am too close and too emotionally attached to this project. Perhaps I need to take a step back and get other perspectives on this issue. Maybe I am overthinking it."

Make responsible decisions. The research on emotional intelligence shows that responsible decision making is the ability to make caring and constructive choices about personal behaviors and social interactions (Goleman, 1995). Although emotionally intelligent leaders listen to dissent, they are not easily persuaded to abandon evidence-based plans—nor do they have an "I'm going to show them" attitude toward our naysayers. Instead, we listen, we question, we evaluate and analyze the appropriate data, and we make the most responsible decision that supports students.

Building Trust Among Skeptics

I have often heard it said that "Your teachers and staff must believe you before they will believe *in* you." To win skeptics over, I have found that three practices are particularly helpful: giving trust, challenging your own mindset, and recognizing the value of the skeptical perspective.

Give trust. Contrary to what some might believe, you gain trust not by earning it but by giving it. Placing your confidence in someone is a deliberate choice. It's also beneficial to your health. Research shows that small, brave acts of choosing trust over cynicism make our brains light up with joy (Angier, 2002). Emotionally intelligent leaders seek to give trust by being transparent, being consistent, extending empathy to others, and taking feedback from others to heart.

Challenge your own mindset. A key step in the process of trust building is to challenge your own mindset when facing skepticism. If you believe that everyone who shows skepticism is automatically wrong, you close down any hope of constructive conversation and collaboration. Behaving in this way will also inevitably create cynics among your team and community members. Challenge yourself to recognize and understand your own emotions, thoughts, and values when skepticism arises. Examine your prejudices and biases.

Recognize the value of the skeptical perspective. Acknowledging the strengths of skeptical arguments allows us to trust those who make them with tasks aligned to those strengths. Skeptics can help us identify the gaps between where we are and where we want to be. Remember that skepticism from your teachers or community members does not necessarily indicate a lack of commitment; some skeptics are just not ready to trust in the future quite yet. That just means they need a little more time to build trust.

Addressing Organized Resistance

Sitting in school board meetings the last few years, I have seen a rise in organized groups demanding accountability from educators. There is power in a collective voice coming to the table demanding change for children. It's important to remember that these voices may sound angry, but not all resistance is bad.

There are two key lessons school leaders should take from organized resisters. First, leaders need to understand *why* parents are organizing in the first place. Listen to and identify the areas of concern being shared. Don't assume you know why parents are organizing. Second, leaders must understand *how* parents and community members organize—what steps they take—so they can identify the signs that a collective is forming. Your role isn't necessarily to stop the organizing but rather to anticipate the concerns that will be brought to your school or board.

There are at least four characteristics of successful collective efforts (Beckwith & Lopez, 1997):

1. They understand that people are motivated by self-interest.
2. The organization is deliberate and thought out, with a leader or set of leaders driving the efforts.
3. Members of the collective are taught to deal with conflict and confrontation. In many organizing efforts, parents and community members will role-play different confrontation scenarios they can expect to encounter.
4. The organizing efforts are purposeful, meaningful, and clear about the concern being addressed.

Underprivileged communities that have been marginalized are particularly primed to manifest their anger and frustration by organizing into one collective voice. Socially aware leaders who can sense frustrations boiling over might organize meetings with key groups to "call in" the issue of contention before it is "called out" at a school board meeting or on social media. In my experience, parents tend to organize when they feel they have not been heard. There will always be signs that parents are starting to organize around school-related concerns, and the more emotional intelligence skills we have, the likelier we will be to see and heed those signs. We can risk the angry mob at our next school board meeting, or we can carve out the time to sit and genuinely listen to the perspectives of others.

Remember that every situation is different. Just because you're facing something similar to what you have seen before doesn't mean that the same solutions or even staff are appropriate. I have seen principals fail to garner the trust from organized groups by saying things like "I've been in education for 30 years, so I've seen this before" or "I know how to handle this situation."

Characteristics of Organized Parent and Community Groups

Programs that train parents and community members to organize appear to be on the rise (National Center for Community Schools, 2021). Such groups often work toward enacting systemwide change focused on such issues as transparency in school finances, parent engagement, school safety, school resource officers, equity, and quality of instruction.

Following are some characteristics of organized parent and community groups. Knowing about these will help you prepare to engage with groups in a way that addresses everyone's concerns:

- **They call out inequities and ineffective practices.** If parent organizations are meeting to discuss inequities related to their students' education, try to attend the meetings or send representatives to listen and answer questions.
- **They build relationships and collective responsibility by identifying shared concerns among families, parents, and community members.** A sudden increase in requests for information from families and parent groups could be a sign of organizing.

- **They choose a leader or leadership team, often through voting.** If you see new leaders or leadership teams being appointed or intense competition for a leadership role, this could be a sign that there is building energy around an issue.
- **They use strategies grounded in adult education, civic engagement, public action, and negotiation to build collective power.** When teachers or community members are reaching out to experts, university professors, or researchers to further explain the data or the history around a topic, this could be a sign that the community is serious about collectively addressing an issue.

Reasons for Organizing

There are three main reasons parent and community groups tend to organize: to address parent or community concerns, to increase leadership development, and to build parent social capital.

Organizing to Address Parent or Community Concerns

People are motivated by issues that directly affect them (Beckwith & Lopez, 1997). Organized groups facilitate the process of issue identification, but parents and community members themselves define the goals. Many groups spring from one-on-one and small-group conversations among parents concerned about a school-related issue. In most cases, the issue is not related to academics but to matters such as health, safety, and bullying. Many groups feel these are "winnable issues" that give parents a sense of their own power to create change. It is much easier, after all, to win on the issue of adding more playground aides than on the issue of recruiting more teachers to reduce class size.

Organizing for Leadership Development

Many groups will invest considerable time and effort on parent leadership development. To develop their knowledge and skills, parent leaders participate in trainings, mentoring sessions, small-group meetings, and public actions. These experiences help them learn more about how school systems work and about school data—knowledge they can leverage to agitate for change. Additionally, parent leadership development can teach parents public speaking skills, research skills, and negotiating tactics.

Organizing to Build Parent Social Capital

Through discussions and small-group gatherings, parents exchange narratives. The exchange of narratives, or stories, fosters empathy between and among individuals, and it encourages parents to offer support to one another. This level of empathetic engagement, in which parents and community members explore common experiences, aspirations for their children, and connections with one another, ultimately enhances social capital. A primary strategy for organizing parents is to create spaces where they can build social capital and then organize different groups of people to grow a larger social network. The organizing world recognizes the concept of "bridging" to link together multiple parent or community groups, with different social capital, to create a broader social network (Gelderblom, 2018; Putnam, 2002).

Conclusion

Leaders can't assume they always know why groups of parents are organizing. When the demonstrations show up, you need to listen and reflect carefully on what the protesters are asking. Don't let the resistance make you anxious, frustrated, or angry. Remember, not all resistance is bad. As a leader, you may be able to leverage these collective voices for positive change. You can also leverage these voices to look within yourself and challenge your own leadership style. Have empathy and understanding but stand your ground when warranted, for the sake of children. Remember that you can't make everyone happy all the time. Pay attention to how decisions are affecting both the internal and external communities. There will be signs when parents and community members start to organize; pay respectful attention to what they have to say.

Reader Reflection

1. What are some examples of ways you have engaged naysayers in your school or community? How did you go about listening to the resistance? How did you navigate your own emotions in those situations?
2. How do you manage your emotions in moments of conflict with naysayers or resisters?
3. Why do you think resisters in your school or community are acting this way?
4. Can you provide examples of when or where you might have enacted the strategies for effectively engaging naysayers discussed in this chapter?
5. Are there other strategies you have used to effectively engage naysayers or resisters in your school? How do you know those strategies were effective?
6. Have you ever felt the need to step back from a situation and get other perspectives on it? Can you explain your

reactions or emotions? Were you able to effectively communicate to your team how you were feeling?

7. What strategies have you used to share your feelings with team members?
8. How would you explain the difference between a naysayer and skeptic? Are there examples from your experiences as a leader or educator you can reference?
9. What goes through your mind when you are working with skeptics in your school or community?
10. What examples can you share of giving trust to skeptics?
11. What signs beyond those discussed in this chapter might suggest that parents or community members are organizing to address school-related issues?
12. Can you provide an example of parents or community groups organizing to address issues of concern in your school or district? How did you navigate these situations? Did you interpret the organizing as resistance?
13. Describe the encounters and interactions you have had with organized groups of parents or community members in your role as a school leader. What were their concerns and what was the outcome?
14. What relationship do you have with existing organizations in your community?

7

Sustaining and Scaling Emotional Intelligence in Schools

While organizing my thoughts for this chapter, I reflected on two school districts navigating similar issues of race and equity. In the first district, Superintendent Abby had seen collective organizing and a growing concern over perceived racist practices in the district. Black students felt unheard and unwelcomed in the district. There were clear achievement gaps between Black and white students, who used the N word loosely without teachers doing anything about it. The district's Black students and teachers demanded greater transparency, more resources for their education, and accountability for teachers and students who broke the district's hate speech policies.

Superintendent Abby took these messages to heart. She began a deep dive into the district's diversity metrics and student success data, hired an equity director, and created a mandatory hate speech curriculum for all 9th graders. She collaborated with the union on designing coaching and intervention plans for navigating hate speech. By all accounts, she started to implement practices that would lead to change and equity in the district. However, after more than a year, the community, students, and faculty were still feeling disconnected. Some improvements were being made, but there was still something missing—a disconnect of sorts. Why? Let me share with you the story of the second district on my mind, and then you'll understand.

The Importance of Taking Ownership

Superintendent Bob had a situation very similar to Abby's. He had crowds of students, parents, and community organizers showing up at board meetings demanding the district fix its achievement gaps. Like Abby, Bob instituted a mandatory hate speech course for all 9th graders. He also analyzed and shared data about the district's spending on Black students, added a new hate speech policy to the student handbook, and provided staff with antiracist and antibias training. He, too, hired a district equity director.

Both Abby and Bob were leaning into their difficult situations, yet Bob was seeing better results, including clearer communication between the administration and students and between the administration and community leaders. He started to attract additional partners from the community and worked with the union to find strategies for closing the achievement gap and creating a welcoming environment for all learners in the district.

So what did Bob do right that Abby didn't? Put simply, he took public ownership of change. When students, parents, and community members showed up at a board meeting to demand action on the achievement gap, Bob addressed them directly. "I am sorry," he said. "I own this as the leader of this district. These equity gaps are on me. If we don't make serious improvement in the next three years, then I will ask the board not to renew my contract." Bob said this out loud, in a public meeting, for all to hear. He then went and met with various student groups, parent groups, community coalitions, and religious leaders and told them the same thing.

Students and families need to hear both that you *as a leader* are taking ownership of the problems in the district and that you *as a person* empathize with them. Change won't happen if the community doesn't believe you really want to fix things. Taking ownership, publicly, courageously, and apologetically is a necessary step toward ensuring the success of any change efforts.

While Superintendent Abby actively listened to the concerns around her, she never showed empathy *as a person*. She never stood up publicly to say, "I own this, it is wrong, and I need to do better." Despite the strategies and policies she implemented, her teachers felt she wasn't genuine in her desire for things to improve because she didn't take any ownership of the problem.

Strategies for Sustaining and Scaling Emotional Intelligence in Schools

In my experience, there are four especially effective strategies leaders can use to sustain and scale emotional intelligence in schools:

1. Owning the hiring process for all staff.
2. Assigning roles to teacher leaders you know can rise to the challenge.
3. Listening actively and intentionally inviting debate.
4. Turning off your ego.

Owning the Hiring Process for All Staff

School leaders need to own all aspects of the hiring process. This means having a line of sight into how hiring committees are formed, helping come up with interview questions, and being a part of interviews. They should feel free to change the hiring committee structures and interview questions as needed to meet the needs of their school. Adding new team members to your community is among the most important decisions a leader can make. It doesn't matter how large or small your school or district is; if you're a principal or superintendent, you need to be involved in the hiring process.

Whether you're hiring a new teacher, receptionist, or custodial staff member, be sure to consider candidates' emotional intelligence. The worst thing leaders can do is hire team members who are later revealed to lack empathy or self-awareness. Ask questions such as these during interviews:

- How would you define and describe emotional intelligence?
- Can you describe the difference between the resources needed to teach students about their emotional intelligence and the resources teachers need to develop their own emotional intelligence?
- How do you respond when a coworker challenges you?
- How do you recover from failure?
- How do you celebrate success?

You can also ask members of the interview committee to answer the same questions they will be posing to candidates.

Research shows that individuals with high EQ are better equipped to cope with challenges and stress, form more meaningful relationships, and exhibit greater social awareness (Orchard et al., 2009). In turn, greater EQ is connected to feeling better about yourself overall (Deci et al., 2001). When we hire team members who feel good about themselves and the work they do, we help create learning environments in which students feel good about themselves.

When sitting in on interviews, listen for responses that speak to the candidate's genuine character. Ask yourself questions such as these:

- Are they communicating positive signs about themselves and their growth? Candidates who own their recent mistakes or failures without blaming others are likely to have high emotional intelligence.
- Do they define the emotions they are experiencing right now in the moment or while discussing a past situation? If so, this speaks to their self-awareness.
- Do they describe having been able to move past challenging situations or emotions in their work? If so, this speaks to their self-management skills.
- Do they discuss having navigated situations by themselves or with peers? In their work, did they take into account other people's suggestions, motivations, or challenges? Listen for how they might have moved past differences or mended relationships. This provides insight into their social awareness and their relationship-building potential as new team members.

Superintendents should engage in some way with all new hires in the district to help set the tone and expectations. No matter how big the district, I would challenge superintendents to schedule time every month or couple of months to meet with new recruits. From teachers to front-office staff to custodial workers, all employees in the district should have a chance to engage with the superintendent.

One leader I know hands out "get out of jail free" cards to all new hires. She uses these cards as an opportunity to challenge them to take risks on behalf of the organization and the success of students. She explains to new hires that she expects them to ask questions and (respectfully) challenge past practices.

Assigning Roles to Teacher Leaders You Know Can Rise to the Challenge

Far too often, the school leaders I work with use the same group of three to five teachers to help them lead the organization. An emotionally intelligent leader knows that assigning leadership opportunities to team members allows not only for their growth but also for the growth of the school or district.

Emotionally intelligent leaders are not jealous leaders; they do not diminish others by saying they can't handle a project or can't lead. Rather, they are multipliers. In her book *Multipliers: How the Best Leaders Make Everyone Smarter*, Liz Wiseman (2010) argues that the best leaders elevate the talent around them by believing in them, trusting them, and inspiring them to take on new challenges and risks together. By creating opportunities for their team members to grow in their own leadership capacities, leaders multiply the leadership workforce in their school or district. Good leaders are always on the lookout for talent in their building that can help carry some of the work forward.

So, how do you spot the emerging leaders in your school? In my experience, there are two different types of emerging leaders in schools. First is the teacher who may be quiet and seem disengaged but in reality fully understands what students need, is aligned with the school's vision and mission, and puts in the extra time to help students. This kind of leader also keeps pace with the change you are trying to bring to the school—they understand the new software system, the shifts in grading policy, the new curriculum adaptations, and so on.

I like to approach this kind of emerging leader with questions about their future career or personal goals. I try to find out as much as I can about what's going on in their lives. Of course, you can't have these conversations unless you have built some relationship with the person. I tend to be pretty direct about asking them to take the lead on a project. Communicating start and end dates is key. I also try to be clear about how leading the project might be beneficial to their own long-term goals. In my experience, these individuals will step up for a season or so before retreating to their classrooms, but they may also reemerge as needed in the future.

The second type of emerging leader is the young, overly wise educator who is proud and thinks they know it all. They have been teaching only a few years but feel they have the command of a veteran. They may get on your nerves a bit, but with the proper coaching and mentoring, they can emerge as solid allies in furthering your vision for the school or district. They also tend to have good stamina and can be helpful in leading projects that require night and weekend engagements.

This type of emerging leader needs a bit more hand-holding than the first. Although you want them to lead projects, you don't want their arrogance to rub other staff the wrong way. To do this, avoid being judgmental and recognize that everyone has different experiences that have shaped their views. In addition, practice active listening and show genuine interest in their perspectives. I review goals and communicate timelines for projects clearly with this type of emerging leader, and I also clearly communicate our plans to the rest of the school community. I showcase the emerging leader in public, thanking them for their work and energy and highlighting results.

Listening Actively and Intentionally Inviting Debate

Sometimes leaders need to shake things up and stir debate to arrive at solutions to challenges. If there are issues you are having trouble reaching a decision on, listen carefully to folks on your team as they propose different viewpoints. If only one perspective is provided, consider splitting your team in half and having them argue for or against a certain proposal.

If you are going to engage in this strategy with your team, you need to set the tone and rules of engagement first. Some teachers may feel uncomfortable arguing for one side over another. I always remind the team that I am just listening for arguments that we may not have thought of to make a more informed decision. Always lay the ground rules for the debate and state the reason why you are doing things this way. Make sure participants don't take the debates personally or attack anyone in their arguments.

Turning Off Your Ego

Scaling the emotional intelligence of your schools requires leaders to check their ego at the door. When things are tough, good leaders without ego know how to step forward and take responsibility for their actions and decisions. When things are going great, they step back and give credit to those around them.

Ego blocks us from improving by telling us that we don't need to improve (Holiday, 2019). It seeks honor, validation, and recognition above all else. Emotional intelligence, by contrast, teaches us to delay gratification and focus on the task at hand regardless of the external recognition we receive. Lack of self-regulation only gets worse when leaders don't check the power of their ego (Liu et al., 2021; Pellitteri, 2002).

Research on emotional intelligence and ego shows that some degree of cognitive reasoning, analysis, and verbal communication skills are needed to be emotionally intelligent (Petrides et al., 2016). These three cognitive factors (reasoning, analysis, and verbal communication) are the same three factors that help us shape, develop, and strengthen our emotional intelligence, yet they are also the same three factors that our ego can highjack in the heat of a turbulent moment or time. In research on the quiet ego, Liu (2022) found that participants who could "quiet their own ego" had especially high emotional intelligence (which the study also found was associated with greater life satisfaction, more positive affect, and less perceived stress).

One way to quiet your ego is to practice mindfulness (Miao et al., 2018). Focus awareness on the present moment and calmly acknowledge your feelings, thoughts, and bodily sensations. Practicing mindfulness helps us cultivate awareness of our surroundings and realign our attitude to be less judgmental and more curious and kind. The best mindfulness strategies are meditation and awareness of breathing. I'm a fan of being outside and going for walks in the forest. I also love to sit and surround myself with music. Other leaders and friends of mine practice yoga or go for long runs to promote mindfulness. Turning off your ego can be an ongoing project.

Knowing When to Leave

It is sadly true that every leader can overstay their welcome in an organization. Emotionally intelligent leaders understand when it's time for them to move on. Leaders who can bring about change, install new assessment practices, or dramatically increase morale don't always stay beyond a couple years. A leader who turns around a school or district, who lifts it out of the gutter, doesn't necessarily have the skills required to sustain these improvements. Organizations reach a point in their development that requires a new mindset, refreshed relationships, and invigorated strategic plans. Sometimes sustaining the work requires fresh eyes.

Some will argue that short leadership tenures undermine the stability of schools, but stability shouldn't rest on the shoulders of the principal or superintendent alone. Emotionally intelligent leaders reach a point where they ask themselves, "Are there others who might be able to do this work better than me?"

Coming to grips with when to leave can be hard for leaders who aren't being encouraged to leave. Such leaders need to rely on their own judgment. Here are some indications that it may be time to start the next chapter in your life:

- Your knowledge base has become static and you find yourself out of sync with changing technologies or ideologies.
- You find yourself losing connections or no longer making new connections among key players in the community and education system.
- You are no longer emotionally engaged with the work.

Finally, make sure to plan for your succession. I don't think schools do a good job of succession planning. You don't want your school or district to wait too long before selecting the next leader. Schools and districts should work with their human resources departments to develop a succession plan and onboarding processes.

Conclusion

Sustaining and scaling the emotional intelligence of our schools takes more than a single leader. It takes a wise and emotionally intelligent community of adults seeking to better themselves and the children they serve. In all my work with education leaders across primary schools, secondary schools, and universities, I have found that emotional intelligence, above all else, is the key to effective education leadership.

Reader Reflection

1. What strategies beyond those mentioned in this chapter have you used to grow and sustain the emotional intelligence of your school community?
2. How might you set the stage for emotionally intelligent interview questions for job candidates?
3. What are some ways you have seen schools or districts successfully hire and onboard new staff?
4. How often does the superintendent in your district check in with principals about the hiring processes?
5. What are your district's practices for calibrating the hiring processes?
6. What are examples of superintendents setting expectations about hiring in your district? Do those

expectations align with efforts to promote a socially and emotionally intelligent school culture?

7. What examples have you used or seen others use for encouraging staff to take risks to benefit students?
8. Can you identify when your ego is starting to get in the way of moving forward?
9. How might you battle with your ego in your own mind?
10. How do you know when you have succeeded in quieting your ego?
11. Can you think of times when you encouraged a teacher or staff member to take on a new leadership role?
12. What are some examples of the types of leadership roles you have assigned teachers or staff who you thought were emerging leaders?
13. Can a leader transitioning out of a building still support the growth of a school community? How so?
14. When should leaders start to think about a succession plan?
15. What does a healthy exit plan look like?

References

Alexander. (2007). 35 dropout factories in CPS. *District 299*. https://district299.typepad.com/district299/2007/10/35-dropout-fact.html

Angier, N. (2002, July 23). Why we're so nice: We're wired to cooperate. *New York Times*. https://www.nytimes.com/2002/07/23/science/why-we-re-so-nice-we-re-wired-to-cooperate.html

Argyris, C. (1990). *Overcoming organizational defenses: Facilitating organizational learning*. Allyn & Bacon.

Baker, W. F., & O'Malley, M. (2008). *Leading with kindness: How good people consistently get superior results*. AMACOM.

Balfanz, R., & Legters, N. (2006). Closing "dropout factories": The graduation-rate crisis we know, and what can be done about it. *Education Week, 25*(42), 42–43.

Bambrick-Santoyo, P. (2010). *Driven by data: A practical guide to improve instruction*. Jossey-Bass.

Bambrick-Santoyo, P. (2012). *Leverage leadership: A practical guide to building exceptional schools*. Jossey-Bass.

Batool, B. F. (2013). Emotional intelligence and effective leadership. *Journal of Business Studies Quarterly, 4*(3), 84.

Beckwith, D., & Lopez, C. (1997). *Community organizing: People power from the grassroots*. University of Wisconsin. http://comm-org.wisc.edu/papers97/beckwith.htm

Bergeron, B. S. (2008). Enacting a culturally responsive curriculum in a novice teacher's classroom. *Urban Education, 43*(1), 4–28.

Bernstein, E., Shore, J., & Lazer, D. (2019). Improving the rhythm of your collaboration. *MIT Sloan Management Review, 61*(2), 29–36.

Bohn, J. (2014). Turning resistant teachers into resilient teachers. *ASCD Express, 9*(10), 1–4.

Bondy, E., Ross, D. D., Gallingane, C., & Hambacher, E. (2007). Creating environments of success and resilience. *Urban Education, 42*, 326–348.

Boudett, P. K., City, A. E., & Murnane, J. R. (2013). *Data wise: A step-by-step guide to using assessment results to improve teaching and learning.* Harvard Education Press.

Bradberry, T., & Greaves, J. (2009). *Emotional intelligence 2.0.* TalentSmart.

Brewer, J. (2021). *Unwinding anxiety: Train your brain to heal your mind.* Vermillion Press.

Brown-Jeffy, S., & Cooper, J. E. (2011). Toward a conceptual framework of culturally relevant pedagogy: An overview of the conceptual and theoretical literature. *Teacher Education Quarterly, 38*(1), 65–84.

Bru-Luna, L. M., Martí-Vilar, M., Merino-Soto, C., & Cervera-Santiago, J. L. (2021, December). Emotional intelligence measures: A systematic review. *Healthcare, 9*(12), 1696.

Bryk, A. S. (2010). Organizing schools for improvement. *Phi Delta Kappan, 91*(7), 23–30.

Cameron, S. K., & Quinn, E. R. (2011). *Diagnosing and changing organizational culture: Based on the competing values framework* (3rd ed.). Jossey-Bass.

Carleton, R. N. (2016). Fear of the unknown: One fear to rule them all? *Journal of Anxiety Disorders, 41*, 5–21.

Chou, E. Y. (2018). Naysaying and negativity promote initial power establishment and leadership endorsement. *Journal of Personality and Social Psychology, 115*(4), 638–656.

City, A. E., Elmore, F. R., Fairman, E. S., & Teitel, L. (2009). *Instructional rounds in education: A network approach to improving teaching and learning.* Harvard Education Press.

Clarke, J., Dede, C., Ketelhut, D. J., & Nelson, B. (2006). A design-based research strategy to promote scalability for educational innovations. *Educational Technology, 46*(3), 27–36.

Collaborative for Academic, Social, and Emotional Learning. (2020a). *CASEL's SEL Framework: What are the core competence areas and where are they promoted?* https://casel.org/casel-sel-framework-11-2020

Collaborative for Academic, Social, and Emotional Learning. (2020b). *Evidence-based social emotional learning programs: CASEL criteria updates and rationale.* https://casel.org/wp-content/uploads/2021/01/11_CASEL-Program-CriteriaRationale.pdf

Coombs, W. T. (2021). *Ongoing crisis communication: Planning, managing, and responding.* Sage.

Cuiccio, C., & Husby-Slater, M. (2018). *Needs assessment guidebook: Supporting the development of district and school needs assessments.* State Support Network.

Deci, E. L., Koestner, R., & Ryan, R. M. (2001). Extrinsic rewards and intrinsic motivation in education: Reconsidered once again. *Review of Educational Research, 71*(1), 1–27.

Deems, R. S., & Deems, T. A. (2003). *Leading in tough times: The manager's guide to responsibility, trust, and motivation*. Human Resource Development Press.

Deeprose, D. (2001). *Making teams work: How to form, measure, and transition today's teams*. American Management Association.

De Smet, A., Rubenstein, K., Schrah, G., Vierow, M., & Edmondson, A. (2021). *Psychological safety and the critical role of leadership development*. https://www.mckinsey.com/capabilities/people-and-organizational-performance/our-insights/psychological-safety-and-the-critical-role-of-leadership-development

Detert, J. R., Seashore Louis, K., & Schroeder, R. G. (2001). A culture framework for education: Defining quality values and their impact in U.S. high schools. *School Effectiveness and School Improvement, 12*(2), 183–212.

Dixon, B. (2012). *Social media for school leaders: A comprehensive guide to getting the most out of Facebook, Twitter, and other essential web tools*. Jossey-Bass.

Dobbin, F., & Kalev, A. (2016). Why diversity programs fail. *Harvard Business Review, 94*(7), 14.

Doe, R., Ndinguri, E., & Phipps, S. T. (2015). Emotional intelligence: The link to success and failure of leadership. *Academy of Educational Leadership Journal, 19*(3), 105.

Donahue-Keegan, D., Villegas-Reimers, E., & Cressey, M. J. (2019). Integrating social-emotional learning and culturally responsive teaching in teacher education preparation programs. *Teacher Education Quarterly, 46*(4), 150–168.

Druskat, V. U., & Wolff, S. B. (2001). Building the emotional intelligence of groups. *Harvard Business Review, 79*(3), 80–91.

Durlak, J. A., Weissberg, R. P., Dymnicki, A. B., Taylor, R. D., & Schellinger, K. B. (2011). The impact of enhancing students' social and emotional learning: A meta-analysis of school-based universal interventions. *Child Development, 82*(1), 405–432.

Easton, L. B. (2009). *Protocols for professional learning*. ASCD.

Elias, M. J., Zins, J. E., Graczyk, P. A., & Weissberg, R. P. (2003). Implementation, sustainability, and scaling up of social-emotional and academic innovations in public schools. *School Psychology Review, 32*(3), 303–319.

Elliott, S. N., & Clifford, M. (2014). *Principal assessment: Leadership behaviors known to influence schools and the learning of all students* (Document No. LS-5). University of Florida, Collaboration for Effective Educator, Development, Accountability, and Reform Center. https://ceedar.education.ufl.edu/wp-content/uploads/2014/09/LS-5_FINAL_09-26-14.pdf

Epstein, J. L. (2019). *School, family, and community partnerships: Your handbook for action*. Corwin Press.

Feyerhem, A., & Rice, C. L. (2002). Emotional intelligence and team performance: The good, the bad, and the ugly. *The International Journal of Organizational Analysis, 10*(4), 343–362.

Friedman, H. S., Riggio, R. E., & Segall, D. O. (1980). Personality and the enactment of emotion. *Journal of Nonverbal Behavior, 1980*(5), 35–48.

Garet, S. M., Porter, C. A., Suk Yoon, K. (2016). What makes professional development effective? Results from a national sample of teachers. *American Education Research Journal, 38*(4). 915–945.

Gay, G. (2010). *Culturally responsive teaching: Theory, research, and practice* (2nd ed.). Teachers College Press.

Gelderblom, D. (2018). The limits to bridging social capital: Power, social context, and the theory of Robert Putnam. *The Sociological Review, 66*(6), 1309–1324.

Gilkey, R., Caceda, R., & Kilts, C. (2010). When emotional reasoning trumps IQ. *Harvard Business Review, 88*(9), 27.

Ginwright, S. A. (2022). *The four pivots: Reimagining justice, reimagining ourselves.* North Atlantic Books.

Goleman, D. (1995). *Emotional intelligence: Why it can matter more than IQ.* Bantam.

Goleman, D. (2014). *What makes a leader: Why emotional intelligence matters.* More Than Sound Publishing.

Goleman, D. (2019). *The emotionally intelligent leader.* Harvard Business School Publishing.

Goleman, D., Boyatzis, R., & McKee, A. (2002). *Primal leadership: Realizing the power of emotional intelligence.* Harvard Business School Press.

Goode, D. T. (2009) *Promoting cultural and linguistic competency.* National Center for Cultural Competence, Georgetown University Center for Child and Human Development. https://nccc.georgetown.edu/documents/ChecklistEIEC.pdf

Greenberg, M. T., Weissberg, R. P., O'Brien, M. U., Zins, J. E., Fredericks, L., Resnik, H., & Elias, M. J. (2003). Enhancing school-based prevention and youth development through coordinated social, emotional, and academic learning. *American Psychologist, 58*(6-7), 466.

Grove, A. S. (1999). *Only the paranoid survive: How to exploit the crisis points that challenge every company.* Currency.

Hammond, Z. (2014). *Culturally responsive teaching and the brain: Promoting authentic engagement and rigor among culturally and linguistically diverse students.* Corwin.

Harrison, E. B., & Mühlberg, J. (2014). *Leadership communication: How leaders communicate and how communicators lead in today's global enterprise.* Business Expert Press.

Haydon, G. (2007). *Values in education.* Continuum Press.

Heers, M., Van Klaveren, C., Groot, W., & Maassen van den Brink, H. (2016). Community schools: What we know and what we need to know. *Review of Educational Research, 86*(4), 1016–1051.

Henderson, A. T., & Mapp, K. L. (2002). *A new wave of evidence: The impact of school, family, and community connections on student achievement.* Annual Synthesis.

Holiday, R. (2019). *Ego is the enemy.* Portfolio.

Horgan, D., & Dimitrijević, B. (2019). Frameworks for citizens participation in planning: From conversational to smart tools. *Sustainable Cities and Society, 48*, 101550.

Howard, G. R. (2016). *We can't teach what we don't know: White teachers, multiracial schools*. Teachers College Press.

Huffington, C., Halton, W., Armstrong, D., & Pooley, J. (2004). *Working below the surface: The emotional life of contemporary organizations*. Routledge.

Humble, J., Molesky, J., & O'Reilly, B. (2015). *Lean enterprise: How high-performance organizations innovate at scale*. O'Reilly Media.

Hyatt, M. (2020). *The vision-driven leader: 10 questions to focus your efforts, energize your team, and scale your business*. Baker.

Ingersoll, R. M. (2001). Teacher turnover and teacher shortages: An organizational analysis. *American Education Research Journal, 38*(3), 499–534.

Ingersoll, R. M. (2003). The wrong solution to teacher shortage. *Educational Leadership, 60*(8), 30–33.

Janis, I. L. (1972). *Victims of groupthink: A psychological study of foreign-policy decisions and fiascoes*. Houghton Mifflin.

Jennings, P. A. (2015). *Mindfulness for teachers: Simple skills for peace and productivity in the classroom*. W. W. Norton & Company.

Jennings, P., Frank, J., & Montgomery, M. (2020). Social and emotional learning for educators. In N. C. Singh & A. Duraiappah (Eds.), *Rethinking learning: A review of social and emotional learning for education systems* (pp. 127–153). https://mgiep.unesco.org/rethinking-learning

Joly, H. (2020). A time to lead with purpose and humanity. *Harvard Business Review, 24*. https://hbr.org/2020/03/a-time-to-lead-with-purpose-and-humanity

Jones, S. M., Brush, K. E., Ramirez, T., Mao, Z. X., Marenus, M., Wettje, S., & Bailey, R. (2021). *Navigating SEL from the inside out: Looking inside & across 33 leading SEL programs: A practical resource for schools and OST providers* (2nd ed.). The EASEL Lab, Harvard Graduate School of Education, and the Wallace Foundation.

Krasnoff, B., Leong, M., & Siebersma, M. (2015). Leadership qualities of effective principals. *Education Northwest, 4*, 1–10.

Krén, H., & Séllei, B. (2021). The role of emotional intelligence in organizational performance. *Periodica Polytechnica Social and Management Sciences, 29*(1), 1–9.

Kruse, S. D., & Louis, K. S. (1993). *An emerging framework for analyzing school-based professional community*. Paper presented at the Annual Meeting of the American Educational Research Association, Atlanta, Georgia. https://files.eric.ed.gov/fulltext/ED358537.pdf

Ladson-Billings, G. (2021). *Culturally relevant pedagogy: Asking a different question*. Teacher College Press.

Ladson-Billings, G. (2023). "Yes, but how do we do it?" Practicing culturally relevant pedagogy. In J. G. Landsman & C. W. Lewis (Eds.), *White teachers/diverse classrooms: Creating inclusive schools, building on students' diversity, and providing true educational equity* (pp. 33–46). Stylus. https://diverseclassconnections.weebly.com/uploads/2/8/5/7/28572651/culturally_relevant.pdf

Landry, L. (2019). Why emotional intelligence is important in leadership. *Harvard Business School Online*. https://online.hbs.edu/blog/post/emotional-intelligence-in-leadership

Lawrence, P. R. (1969). How to deal with resistance to change. *Harvard Business Review*. https://hbr.org/1969/01/how-to-deal-with-resistance-to-change

Liu, G. (2022). Quiet ego and well-being: The what, why, and how—an investigation of the implications of the quiet ego for psychological well-being (Doctoral dissertation). https://scholarworks.umass.edu/dissertations_2/2454

Liu, G., Isbell, L. M., & Leidner, B. (2021). Quiet ego and subjective well-being: The role of emotional intelligence and mindfulness. *Journal of Happiness Studies, 22*, 2599–2619.

Lopez, I. (2017). *Keeping it real and relevant: Building authentic relationships in your diverse classroom*. ASCD.

Lopez, M. E. (2003). *Transforming schools through community organizing: A research review*. Harvard Family Research Project.

Mandell, B., & Pherwani, S. (2003). Relationship between emotional intelligence and transformational leadership style: A gender comparison. *Journal of Business and Psychology, 17*, 387–404.

Markey, M. (2018, September 18). How to increase emotional intelligence on your team. *Forbes*. https://www.forbes.com/sites/forbeshumanresourcescouncil/2018/09/18/how-to-increase-emotional-intelligence-on-your-team

Markowitz, L. N., & Bouffard, M. S. (2020). *Teaching with a social, emotional, and cultural lens: A framework for educators and teacher educators*. Harvard Education Press.

Maslansky, M. (2010). *The language of trust: Selling ideas in a world of skeptics*. Wiley.

McCallops, K., Barnes, T. N., Berte, I., Fenniman, J., Jones, I., Navon, R., & Nelson, M. (2019). Incorporating culturally responsive pedagogy within social-emotional learning interventions in urban schools: An international systematic review. *International Journal of Educational Research, 94*, 11–28.

McGraw Hill. (2019). Social and emotional learning is for teachers, too. *Medium*. https://medium.com/inspired-ideas-prek-12/social-and-emotional-learning-is-for-teachers-too-55aaf1556c57

McKee, A., Boyatzis, R. E., & Johnston, F. (2008). *Becoming a resonant leader: Develop your emotional intelligence, renew your relationships, sustain your effectiveness*. Harvard Business Press.

Miao, C., Humphrey, R. H., & Qian, S. (2018). The relationship between emotional intelligence and trait mindfulness: A meta-analytic review. *Personality and Individual Differences, 135*, 101–107.

Murphy, F. (2013). *Community engagement, organization, and development for public health practice*. Springer.

National Center for Community Schools. (2021). *Building community schools: A guide to action*. Author. https://www.nccs.org/wp-content/uploads/2021/10/NCCS_BuildingCommunitySchools.pdf

National Education Goals Panel. (1998). *Community organizing guide: A framework for the development of systemic reform.* U.S. Government Printing Office. https://govinfo.library.unt.edu/negp/reports/orguide.pdf

Orchard, B., MacCann, C., Schulze, R., Matthews, G., Zeidner, M., & Roberts, R. D. (2009). New directions and alternative approaches to the measurement of emotional intelligence. *Assessing Emotional Intelligence: Theory, Research, and Applications,* 321–344.

Overby, S. (2020, June 1). *Emotional intelligence: 10 ways to manage emotions in a crisis.* The Enterprisers Project. https://enterprisersproject.com/article/2020/6/emotional-intelligence-how-manage-emotions

OWP/P Architects, VS Furniture, & Bruce Mau Design. (2010). *The third teacher: 79 ways you can use design to transform teaching and learning.* Abrams.

Page, S. (2008). *The difference: How the power of diversity creates better groups, firms, schools, and societies.* Princeton University Press.

Paine, S., & McCann, R. (2009). Engaging stakeholders: Including parents and the community to sustain improved reading outcomes. *Sustaining Reading First, 6,* 1–16.

Parekh, N. P. (2003). When nice guys finish first: The evolution of cooperation, the study of law, and the ordering of legal regimes. *University of Michigan Journal of Law Reform, 37,* 909.

Parrish, P., & Linder-VanBerschot, J. (2010). Cultural dimensions of learning: Addressing the challenges of multicultural instruction. *The International Review of Research in Open and Distributed Learning, 11*(2), 1–19.

Payne, C. M. (2008). *So much reform, so little change: The persistence of failure in urban schools.* Harvard University Press.

Pellitteri, J. (2002). The relationship between emotional intelligence and ego defense mechanisms. *The Journal of Psychology, 136*(2), 182–194.

Petrides, K. V., Mikolajczak, M., Mavroveli, S., Sanchez-Ruiz, M. J., Furnham, A., & Pérez-González, J. C. (2016). Developments in trait emotional intelligence research. *Emotion Review, 8*(4), 335–341.

Phillips, K. W., Medin, D., Lee, C. D., Bang, M., Bishop, S., & Lee, D. N. (2014). How diversity works. *Scientific American, 311*(4), 42–47.

Phillips, K. W., Northcraft, G. B., & Neale, M. A. (2006). Surface-level diversity and decision-making in groups: When does deep-level similarity help? *Group Processes & Intergroup Relations, 9*(4), 467–482.

Phuntsog, N. B. (2001). Culturally responsive teaching: What do selected United States elementary school teachers think? *Intercultural Education, 12*(1), 51–64.

Porter, J., & Gallo, A. (2016). How to handle the naysayer on your team. *Harvard Business Review.* https://hbr.org/2016/03/how-to-handle-the-naysayer-on-your-team

Putnam, R. D. (2002). *Bowling alone.* Free Press.

Riddell, R. (2013). Chicago board of education to shut down 50 schools. *K–12 Dive.* https://www.k12dive.com/news/chicago-board-of-education-to-shut-down-50-schools

Ripley, A. (2021). *High conflict: Why we get trapped and how we get out*. Simon and Schuster.

Ronfeldt, M., Farmer, S., McQueen, K., & Grissom, J. (2015). Teacher collaboration in instructional teams and student achievement. *American Educational Research Journal, 52*(3), 475–514.

Safir, S., & Dugan, J. (2021). *Street data: A next-generation model for equity, pedagogy, and school transformation*. Corwin.

Salovey, P., Mayer, J. D., Caruso, D., & Yoo, S. H. (2009). The positive psychology of emotional intelligence. In S. J. Lopez & C. R. Snyder (Eds.), *The Oxford handbook of positive psychology* (2nd ed.). (pp. 237–248). Oxford University Press.

Sandler, C. (2009). The psychological role of the leader in turbulent times. *Strategic HR Review, 8*(3), 30–35. 8

Schlauch, C. R. (2015). Readings of Winnicott. *Pastoral Psychology, 65*, 255–281.

Simmons, N. D. (2019). You can't be emotionally intelligent without being culturally responsive: Why FCS must employ both to meet the needs of our nation. *Journal of Family and Consumer Sciences, 111*(2), 7–16.

Slochower, J. (2013). Relational holding: Using Winnicott today. *Romanian Journal of Psychoanalysis, 6*(2). 2–27.

Snyder, R. R. (2017). Resistance to change among veteran teachers: Providing voice for more effective engagement. *International Journal of Educational Leadership Preparation, 12*(1), n1.

Tang, Y. Y., & Tang, R. (2020). *The neuroscience of meditation: Understanding individual differences*. Academic Press.

Topchik, G. S. (2007). *The first-time manager's guide to team building*. AMACOM.

Topor, D. R., Keane, S. P., Shelton, T. L., & Calkins, S. D. (2010). Parent involvement and student academic performance: A multiple mediational analysis. *Journal of Prevention & Intervention in the Community, 38*(3), 183–197.

Tran, H., Smith, D. A., & Buckman, D. G. (2019). *Stakeholder engagement: Improving education through multi-level community relations*. Rowman & Littlefield.

Tversky, A., & Kahneman, D. (2003). *Judgement under uncertainty: Heuristics and biases*. Cambridge University Press.

Ugoani, J., Amu, C., & Emenike, K. O. (2015). Dimensions of emotional intelligence and transformational leadership: A correlation analysis. *Independent Journal of Management & Production, 6*, 1–22.

Vescio, V., Ross, D., & Adams, A. (2008). A review of research on the impact of professional learning communities on teaching practice and student learning. *Teaching and Teacher Education, 24*(1), 80–91.

Vinovskis, M. (2015). *From A Nation at Risk to No Child Left Behind: National education goals and the creation of federal education policy*. Teachers College Press.

Walker, A. (2012). Leaders seeking resonance: Managing the connectors that bind schools. *International Journal of Leadership in Education, 15*(2), 237–253.

Ware, F. (2006). Warm demander pedagogy: Culturally responsive teaching that supports a culture of achievement for African American students. *Urban Education, 41*(4), 427–456.

Wei, X., Liu, Y., & Allen, N. J. (2016). Measuring team emotional intelligence: A multimethod comparison. *Group Dynamics: Theory, research, and practice, 20*(1), 34.

Wiseman, L. (2010). *Multipliers: How the best leaders make everyone smarter.* Harper Business.

Zins, J. E., Bloodworth, M. R., Weissberg, R. P., & Walberg, H. J. (2007). The scientific base linking social and emotional learning to school success. *Journal of Educational and Psychological Consultation, 17*(2-3), 191–210.

Index

The letter *f* following a page locator denotes a figure.

achievement, desire for, 12–13
assumptions, challenging for culture change, 51–52

beliefs, challenging for culture change, 51–52

caring norms, 45
communication
    pacing strategies, 35–36
    stakeholder, 69–70
    in times of crisis, 19–22
communication plans and structures, 31, 35–36
community, vision planning and, 31–32
community groups, organized, 85–87
community-school relationships, trends in, 67
conflict vs. unity in institutional design, 3
confrontation norms, 44–45
crisis, leadership in times of, 18–22
cultural responsiveness, 15–16, 17*f*, 18
culture. *See* school culture

debate, inviting, 97
disorganization, controlled, 47
dissent. *See* naysayers and resisters
ego, turning off one's, 97–98
emotional intelligence (EQ)
    advantages to people with high, 93–94
    benefits of, 2–3
    developing, 15–16
    dimensions of, 3
    strengthening, 98
    vignette illustrating lack of, 1–2
emotional security, values in, 54–55
emotions. *See also* self-awareness; self-regulation
    controlling, 10–12, 81
    influencing others,' 20–21
empathy
    in culturally responsive work, 17*f*
    introduction to, 13–14
    public, 92
engagement norms, 52
engagement protocols, 69–70

events, themed, 35–36
experiences, culture change through shared, 52

feedback for self-awareness, 11
friends, relying on for self-awareness, 11

groups, EQ. *See* teams, EQ

hiring process, owning the, 93–95
holding space, 19–20

influencer stakeholders, 68
institutional design, conflict vs. unity in, 3
instructional leadership team (ILT), 24–25

leaders, EQ. *See also specific characteristics*
    characteristics, 4–5, 20–21, 51, 91–92, 95, 99
    communication skills, 21–22
    culturally responsive, 15–16, 17*f*, 18
    ego, 97–98
    holding space, 19–20
    knowing when to leave, 99–100
leadership
    behaviors for navigating challenges, 18–22
    of EQ groups, 42–45
    fire vignette, 18–19
    vision and, 24–25
leadership development, organizing for, 87
listening, active, 13, 97
looping, 13

meditation for self-awareness, 11
meeting norms, 52
mindfulness, 98
minding your mood, 20–21
mindset, values and a calibrated, 54–55

mission statements vs. vision statements, 25–27, 26*f*
mood, minding your, 20–21
motivation, 12–13

naysayers and resisters
    benefits of, 79–81, 83
    building trust, 82–83
    engaging using EQ, 79–82
    interpreting, 78
    introduction to, 77–78
    organized, 83–87
norms
    caring, 45
    confrontation, 44–45
    creating EQ, 42–43
    interpersonal understanding, 43–44
    meeting and engagement, 52
    perspective-taking, 44

obligation stakeholders, 68
ownership, importance of taking public, 91–92

parent groups, organized, 85–87
partnerships, stakeholder, 66
passion, principle over, 36–37
perspective, broadening, 13
perspective-taking norms, 44
power, dissent and the endowment of, 79–80
principal's corner, 35
principle over passion, 36–37
professional learning, protocols for, 36
proximity stakeholders, 69

quiet, scheduling for, 35

recruitment, teacher, 54, 93–95
relationships. *See* empathy; social skills
reliance stakeholders, 69
representation stakeholders, 69
resisters. *See* naysayers and resisters
retention, teacher, 54

school culture
　displaying evidence of, 53
　EQ, strategies for shaping, 51–52
　positive, benefits of, 50
　strength, components of, 50–51
　values-aligned, creating a, 56–59, 60–61*f*, 62–63
　values in, 51
schools
　cultural responsiveness, 15–16, 17*f*, 18
　strategies for sustaining and scaling EQ in, 92–100
　system anxiety, 19
self-awareness
　in addressing dissent, 78, 79, 81–82
　building, methods of, 11
　in culturally responsive work, 17*f*
　introduction to, 10–11
self-regulation, 11–12, 81
silence, scheduling for, 35
social-emotional learning (SEL), 9–10
social skills, 14–15
space, holding, 19–20
stakeholders, engaging external
　case study, 71–74
　codesigning protocols of engagement, 70
　communication among groups, 69–70
　community-school relationships, trends in, 67
　components key to, 67–68
　expectations for successful, 66
　following through on commitments to, 70–71
　identifying groups for, 68–69
　ownership to encourage, 71
　process, 65–66
　repeating vision when, 69
　successfully, 74

teacher leaders, developing, 95–97
teachers
　owning the hiring process for, 93–95

teachers (*continued*)
　values in attracting and retaining, 54
　in vision statements, 28–29
teams, emotionally incompetent, 43–44
teams, EQ
　controlled disorganization in, 47
　effective, characteristics of, 41–42
　high-stakes thinking, 46–47
　incubating, 46–48
　leadership, 48
　norms of, 42–45
thinking, high-stakes, 46–47
town hall meetings, 35
transparency for stakeholder engagement, 66
trust, building with skeptics, 82–83

values
　case study, 55–59, 60–61*f*, 62–63
　in culture change, 53
　importance of, 53–55
　reinforcing, 51
vision
　articulating, 25
　communicating to stakeholders, 69
　confusing, 33–34
　intuitive, 34
　leadership and, 24–25
　repeating, importance of, 34–35
　vague, 33
vision planning components
　communication plans and structures, 31, 69
　measuring impact on others, 31–32
　school programs, 30
　teachers and teacher teams in, 28–29
vision statements
　assessing clarity of, 32–34
　effective, focus areas of an, 28–32
　mission statements vs., 25–27, 26*f*

About the Author

Ignacio Lopez is an educational psychologist, author, and leader focused on supporting the development of educators and education organizations that embrace inclusive, emotionally intelligent, and culturally relevant learning environments. In his writing, Lopez provides helpful, relevant, and research-based leadership and instructional strategies that help educators challenge their own mindsets and practices toward advancing the academic and social emotional lives of the students they serve.

Over his 20-year education career, Lopez has served as a district advisor, consultant, and researcher in collaboration with several school districts throughout the United States. He has been a high school teacher, administrator, college dean, community college president, and elected school board member in Illinois. Lopez is the author of several articles and of the 2017 ASCD book *Keeping It Real and Relevant: Building Authentic Relationships in Your Diverse Classroom.*

Related ASCD Resources: Emotional Intelligence

At the time of publication, the following resources were available (ASCD stock numbers in parentheses).

Becoming a Globally Competent School Leader by Ariel Tichnor-Wagner (#119011)

From Stressed Out to Stress Wise: How You and Your Students Can Navigate Challenges and Nurture Vitality by Abby Wills, Anjali Deva, and Niki Saccareccia (#123004)

Illuminate the Way: The School Leader's Guide to Addressing and Preventing Teacher Burnout by Chase Mielke (#123032)

Keeping It Real and Relevant: Building Authentic Relationships in Your Diverse Classroom by Ignacio Lopez (#117049)

Leadership for Learning: How to Bring Out the Best in Every Teacher, 2nd Edition, by Carl Glickman and Rebecca West Burns (#121007)

The Principal as Chief Empathy Officer: Creating a Culture Where Everyone Grows by Thomas R. Hoerr (#122030)

Taking Social-Emotional Learning Schoolwide: The Formative Five Success Skills for Students and Staff by Thomas R. Hoerr (#120014)

For up-to-date information about ASCD resources, go to www.ascd.org. You can search the complete archives of *Educational Leadership* at www.ascd.org/el. To contact us, sent an email to member@ascd.org or call 800-933-2723 or 703-578-9600.

WHOLE CHILD
TENETS

1 HEALTHY
Each student enters school **healthy** and learns about and practices a healthy lifestyle.

2 SAFE
Each student learns in an environment that is physically and emotionally **safe** for students and adults.

3 ENGAGED
Each student is actively **engaged** in learning and is connected to the school and broader community.

4 SUPPORTED
Each student has access to personalized learning and is **supported** by qualified, caring adults.

5 CHALLENGED
Each student is **challenged** academically and prepared for success in college or further study and for employment and participation in a global environment.

ascd whole child

The ASCD Whole Child approach is an effort to transition from a focus on narrowly defined academic achievement to one that promotes the long-term development and success of all children. Through this approach, ASCD supports educators, families, community members, and policymakers as they move from a vision about educating the whole child to sustainable, collaborative actions.

The EQ Way relates to the **safe** and **supported** tenets.

For more about the ASCD Whole Child approach, visit **www.ascd.org/wholechild.**

Become an ASCD member today!
Go to www.ascd.org/joinascd
or call toll-free: 800-933-ASCD (2723)

DON'T MISS A SINGLE ISSUE OF ASCD'S AWARD-WINNING MAGAZINE.

ascd educational leadership

If you belong to a Professional Learning Community, you may be looking for a way to get your fellow educators' minds around a complex topic. Why not delve into a relevant theme issue of *Educational Leadership*, the journal written by educators for educators?

Subscribe now, or purchase back issues of ASCD's flagship publication at **www.ascd.org/el**. Discounts on bulk purchases are available.

To see more details about these and other popular issues of *Educational Leadership*, visit **www.ascd.org/el/all**.

2800 Shirlington Road
Suite 1001
Arlington, VA 22206 USA

www.ascd.org/learnmore